BASEBALL'S
GREATEST RIVALRIES

The most fearsome feuds and memorable confrontations in Major League history.

Baseball Insiders Library™

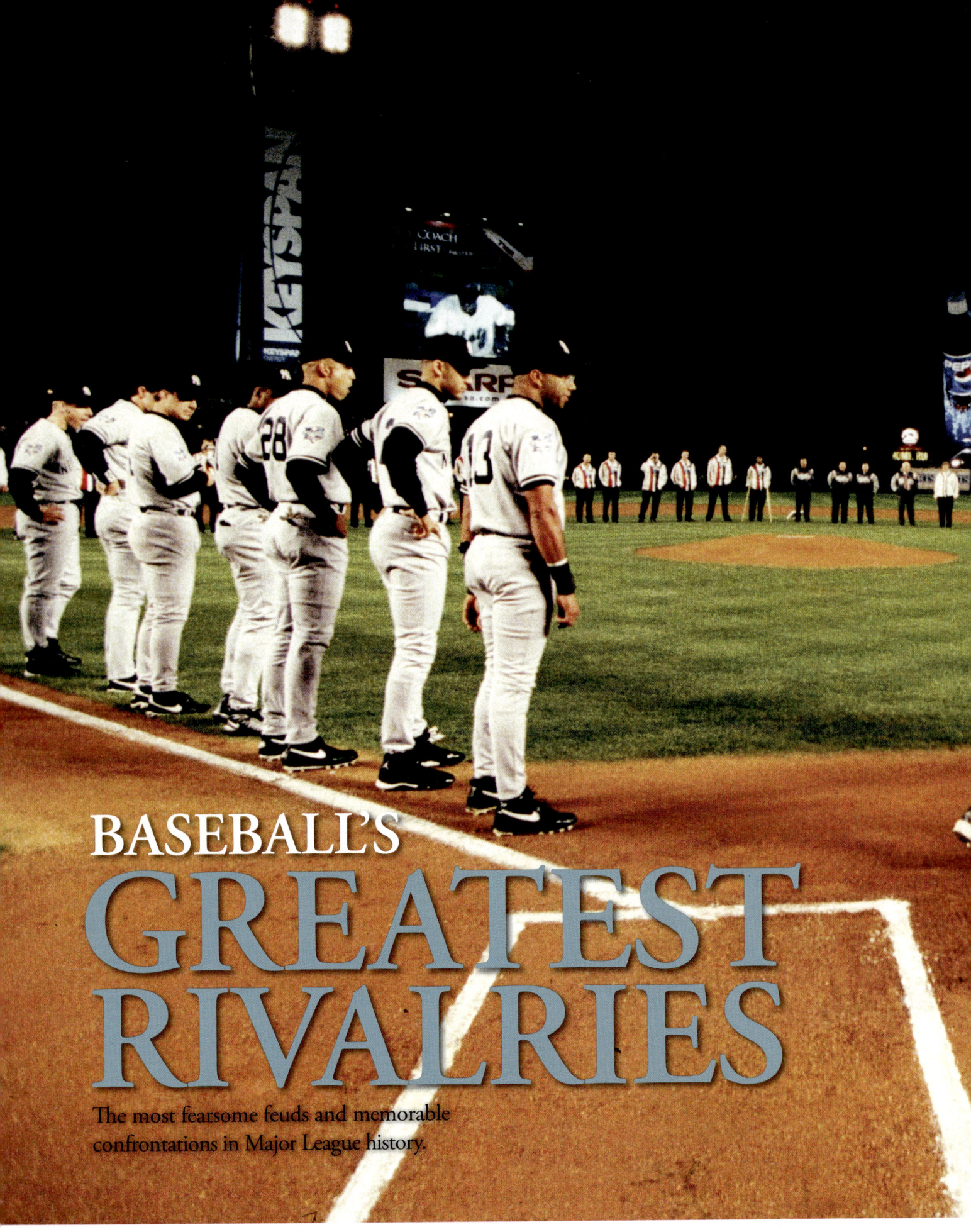

BASEBALL'S GREATEST RIVALRIES

The most fearsome feuds and memorable confrontations in Major League history.

BASEBALL'S GREATEST RIVALRIES by Troy E. Renck
The most fearsome feuds and memorable confrontations in Major League history.

Printed in 2011

About the Author
Troy E. Renck has covered Major League Baseball and the Colorado Rockies since 1996. He has been at the Denver Post *since 2002, and has served as the national and beat writer since 2006. Renck has written* Baseball's Greatest Personalities, *in the* Baseball Insiders Library™ *and is also a regular contributor on ESPN's "First Take" Doubleheader segment. He lives in Longmont, Colo., with his wife and two sons.*

Acknowledgements
Major League Baseball would like to thank Pat Kelly and Milo Stewart Jr. at the National Baseball Hall of Fame and Museum for their invaluable assistance; as well as Eric Enders and David Jones for their diligent work in helping to prepare the book for publication.

Major League Baseball Properties

Vice President, Publishing
Donald S. Hintze

Editorial Director
Mike McCormick

Publications Art Director
Faith M. Rittenberg

Senior Production Manager
Claire Walsh

Managing Editor
Jon Schwartz

Project Associate Art Director
Mark Calimbas

Senior Publishing Coordinator
Anamika Panchoo

Project Editor
Chris Greenberg

Project Assistant Editors
Paul Boye, Allison Duffy

Editorial Interns
Nick Carroll, Bill San Antonio

Major League Baseball Photos

Director
Rich Pilling

Photo Editor
Jessica Foster

Assistant Photo Editor
Charlotte Brown

MLB Insiders Club

Managing Editor
Jen Weaverling

Art Director
Brian Peterson

Proofreader
Travis Bullinger

1 2 3 4 5 6 7 8 9 10 / 15 14 13 12 11

Copyright © MLB Insiders Club 2011

ISBN: 978-1-58159-538-3

All rights reserved. No part of this publication may be reproduced, stored in an electronic retrieval system or transmitted in any form or by any means (electronic, photocopying, recording or otherwise) without the prior or written permission of the copyright owner.

MLB Insiders Club
12301 Whitewater Drive
Minnetonka, MN 55343

TABLE OF CONTENTS

Introduction		6
Chapter 1	Red Sox–Yankees	8
Chapter 2	Trash Talk	32
Chapter 3	Cubs-Cardinals	44
Chapter 4	Man to Man	58
Chapter 5	Yankees-Dodgers	80
Chapter 6	Playoff Rivals	94
Chapter 7	World Series Rivals	108
Chapter 8	Short-Term Rivalries	120
Chapter 9	Dodgers-Giants	138
Source Notes		156
Credits/Index		158

INTRO

According to *Merriam-Webster's Dictionary*, the first known use of the word "rivalry" occurred in 1598. The word was derived from the same linguistic family as the verb "compete" and was frequently used in regards to economics and provincial conflict. Perhaps back then, the giants of Brobdingnag and the Lilliputians were bigger rivals than baseball's Giants and Dodgers are today. But it's unlikely. At their essence, sports are about competition, about keeping score and a record of those results. Since baseball's earliest days, teams have fought over territory (like the Giants, Dodgers and Yankees), over players (like the Philadelphia Phillies and Athletics in early 1900s), and for victories.

There's no single recipe for a great rivalry. Sometimes, the best are player against player. Who can forget the memorable showdowns between the Yankees' Goose Gossage and the Royals' George Brett, with American League supremacy hanging in the balance? Or the summer showdown between pitchers Smoky Joe Wood and Walter Johnson? Sometimes, executives create the crossfire. After the Brooklyn Dodgers' leadership fractured, Larry MacPhail and Branch Rickey tried to make each other miserable, a feud that featured skipper Leo Durocher as an unlikely pawn.

Superstar players can catalyze a feud, but the rivalry itself is bigger than them. An important test of this is the passion of the

fanbases. As a mutual dislike matures, fans develop such deep connections that they take as much pleasure in their enemy's losses as their own team's victories. It becomes personal.

Colorful language spices up any rivalry, too. Like when Giants' Manager John McGraw picked a fight with Connie Mack's 1904 Athletics, laughing them off as "white elephants." Mack created an elephant insignia to mock his new foe. Or when Babe Ruth allegedly called his shot after the Cubs razzed him from their bench, prodding the game's greatest slugger into action.

Along the way, enduring conflicts deliver memorable moments that turn a packed stadium into a human goosebump — Bobby Thomson's 'Shot Heard 'Round the World,' for instance. Or they cause thousands of stunned fans to groan in unison a la Bucky Dent. Some rivalries are born from such October memories.

Rivalries are what "stir the drink" of baseball, as Reggie Jackson might say. They provide the tension that fills the space between games, between at-bats and between pitches; the vitriol felt by opposing fans toward each other as their favorite clubs vie for the same prize; the ultimate gratification that comes each time a rival is bested. These are the things that keep baseball the beautiful game it has always been, and color its past with vibrant tales of foes old and new on the path to the World Series.

Ruth

chapter 1
RED SOX–YANKEES

Boxing has Ali-Frazier. There's Duke–North Carolina in college hoops and Michigan–Ohio State on the gridiron. But perhaps the most fascinating rivalry in sports is between the New York Yankees and the Boston Red Sox. The generations-old feud is rooted in the provincial pride of these northeastern cities that lie less than 200 miles apart. Since an infamously ill-conceived player transaction in 1919, the Yankees have won nearly 30 world titles. The Red Sox haven't come close, but who's counting? As the teams have been very evenly matched in recent years, the rivalry has only become more intense. Red Sox President Larry Lucchino summed up Boston's feelings toward the Yankees back in 2002, calling the club "The Evil Empire." "I didn't start the rivalry," Lucchino said. "I just threw a can of kerosene on the fire."

THE OPENING ACT

There was never a limit with Red Sox Owner Harry Frazee, who managed to alter the course of two iconic franchises during his tumultuous stewardship of Boston's American League club from 1916 to 1923. He delighted in excess of all kinds, reveling in the glow of the spotlight — and the footlights.

As *Boston Globe* sports columnist Dan Shaughnessy explained in his 1990 book *The Curse of the Bambino*, Frazee's lavish tastes and outsized ambition created chronic financial problems. The brazen Broadway producer always needed fresh revenue streams to keep his enterprises afloat. After Boston won the World Series in 1918, Frazee unwittingly launched the Red Sox–Yankees rivalry by selling Ruth to New York on Dec. 26, 1919, for $100,000 up front and the promise of a $300,000 loan. The transaction merely ruined the next 86 Christmases for Red Sox fans.

At that time, it was the largest sum ever paid for a baseball player. Nevertheless, Ruth became a bargain over the years. After pitching to a 78-40 record for the Red Sox from 1915–18, Ruth evolved into the game's premier slugger while playing in New York. The sale effectively ended Boston's mini-dynasty of four World Series triumphs in seven seasons. With Ruth in the fold, New York would become a World Series fixture, winning 26 world titles in the next 86 years, leading many to wonder if Frazee's folly had indeed cursed the club.

Superstitions aside, Ruth remains at the center of the rivalry and, nearly six decades after he took off his Sox, one of sport's most iconic figures.

RED SOX–YANKEES

Hoyt

ONE-WAY STREET

When Boston Owner Harry Frazee, attempting to fund his lavish lifestyle, shopped Babe Ruth to the Yankees, it changed everything about the burgeoning rivalry. Ruth became arguably the greatest player ever, synonymous with "The Curse" that hung over Boston for the next eight-plus decades. Truth is, Ruth had a lot of help with that alleged voodoo. Once Frazee found a willing partner anxious to swap cash for talent, the trade corridors opened between the two franchises. Several key components of the Boston club were dealt, including pitchers Carl Mays and Waite Hoyt. The right-handed Hoyt would go on to win 155 games with the Yankees from 1921–29, including 23 in 1928. "Jumpin" Joe Dugan was added at third base. Hall of Famer Red Ruffing was traded to New York in the '30s, helping the Yankees keep a stranglehold on world titles.

These weren't trades so much as steals, a series of one-sided deals between the two franchises. Frazee signed off on the deals of Mays and Hoyt, who, along with Ruffing, Ruth and Gehrig, became central figures of the Yankees' dynasties in the '20s and '30s. Frazee became the modern-day inventor of the fire sale. Without a commissioner who was willing to nix the lopsided deals, he used the Yankees as his personal ATM as the Red Sox embarked down a torturous road of title-less seasons.

FIRST CUT IS THE DEEPEST

The first time Boston and New York dueled for a pennant was in 1904, just the fourth year of play for the fledgling American League. The Red Sox were known as the Americans. The Yankees were the Highlanders, having just moved to Hilltop Park in Washington Heights, N.Y., after two seasons in Baltimore.

The Highlanders' owner had little confidence that his club would be in the race and had leased his stadium for a Columbia University football game on Saturday, Oct. 8. A century later, it would seem *fait accompli* that New York and Boston would be embroiled in late-season drama, but in 1904, renting out the park seemed a savvy business move. After New York won the opener of the five-game series behind pitcher "Happy" Jack Chesbro, the teams traveled up to Boston's Huntington Avenue Grounds for a doubleheader the next day. After Boston took both games, the rivals traveled back to New York for a season-ending doubleheader.

Chesbro was a horse before the term entered into the baseball lexicon. He went 41-12 with 48 complete games. His tally of 41 regular-season victories remains an AL single-season record, and no player has gotten within 10 wins of that sum since Denny McLain notched 31 in 1968. After leaning on Chesbro — who even made a handful of relief appearances — all season long, the Highlanders looked to him to deliver his best performance on the final day of the campaign. The Highlanders needed to sweep a doubleheader to win the pennant and Chesbro got the ball in game 1. The taut affair was tied, 2-2, entering the ninth. In that fateful, final frame, Chesbro unleashed a wild pitch — a misbehaving but legal spitball — that gave the Americans the win and the pennant. It was their first of five titles over the next 15 years. Chesbro would continue pitching for the Highlanders until 1909, when he would head north to Boston for his last professional season.

Chesbro

RED SOX–YANKEES

RIDING TALL

By 1996, Red Sox fans were defined by their angst. Near misses in 1986, 1975 and 1946 had made baseball heartbreak a generational rite of passage in the Hub. During the decade after the team came within a single strike of winning the '86 World Series against the New York Mets, the club had made just three postseason trips. Seemingly little had gone right since that ground ball got by Bill Buckner at first base. Still, the losing never got any easier for either the team or its fans, especially since the Yankees won 26 World Series rings before Boston ended its title drought.

In any longstanding conflict, there are few characters that inflict more pain than those who change allegiances. After playing the first 11 years of his Hall of Fame career with the Red Sox, Wade Boggs signed a three-year free-agent deal with the Yankees before the 1993 season. Already a five-time batting champ when he first donned pinstripes, Boggs would rebound from a lackluster '92 campaign in Boston to rake at a .313 clip during his five seasons in New York while earning a pair of Gold Gloves for his play at third base. Spending much of the 1996 season atop the Yankees' batting order, Boggs was a key cog in the lineup that got the Bombers back to the Fall Classic for the first time since 1981.

When the Yankees roared back from a 2-games-to-none deficit against the Atlanta Braves to win the World Series in 1996, Boggs provided one of the enduring images of the raucous celebration in the Big Apple — New York's first baseball title since the crosstown Mets had dispatched Boggs and the Sox in 1986. The image of Boggs' celebratory post-game gallop aboard a police officer's horse was enough to make Boston fans ill. "I'm deathly afraid of horses. I just did it. It felt great. This is what I've been waiting for," Boggs said.

BOGGS' STATS WITH THE RED SOX AND YANKEES						
Team	G	R	H	HR	RBI	AVG
Red Sox	1,625	1,067	2,098	85	687	.338
Yankees	602	355	702	24	246	.313

Boggs

RED SOX–YANKEES

McCarthy (left), Williams

ENCORE

Decades before Yankees Owner George Steinbrenner spared no expense to build a championship roster, Red Sox patriarch Tom Yawkey provided the blueprint — and the bank roll. Prior to the 1948 campaign, Yawkey went all in.

Yawkey's free-spending, World Series-or-bust ways were highlighted by the hiring of retired Yankees skipper Joe McCarthy. He lured McCarthy, owner of seven world titles, out of retirement with the goal of winning a World Series in Boston. Yawkey secured top-of-the-rotation pitchers, including Jack Kramer and Ellis Kinder. McCarthy's '48 club won 96 regular-season games. With Ted Williams leading the charge, Boston led the American League in runs scored by a margin of 50 over the second-place club (the Yankees, fittingly). But even the efforts of the Yankees' most successful field general could not lift the "Curse of the Bambino." Boston lost out on the pennant in a one-game playoff with the Cleveland Indians.

Led by a stellar pitching staff that featured Bob Feller, Bob Lemon and Gene Bearden — who earned the win in that pivotal playoff game — the Tribe would go on to top the Boston Braves in the World Series. McCarthy returned to Fenway for the '49 season, again leading the Sox to 96 victories, only to have New York steal the AL pennant on the final day of the season.

"I am physically tired, physically exhausted," said the downtrodden McCarthy when he stepped down a second time.

Yogi Berra (sliding), Bobby Doerr (5)

LAST-MINUTE HEROICS

The history of the Red Sox–Yankees rivalry is defined by equal passion on both sides of the divide, but it has not always featured equal talent and wire-to-wire races. While the teams and their fans use each other as a measuring stick, their regular-season matchups have sometimes lacked tension. But from 1948–50, the palpable pennant race drama was ready for Hollywood.

In 1949, the Red Sox arrived at Yankee Stadium for a two-game series during the last weekend of the regular season. Boston held a one-game lead in the standings. Little-known Yankees outfielder Johnny Lindell shocked Boston in the first game with an eighth-inning home run for the win. "It's all Joe McCarthy's fault," Lindell said of the Red Sox manager, who previously led New York to seven titles before taking over in Boston. "When I came up with the Yankees, he switched me to the outfield."

Even though he might not have still been in the Majors without McCarthy's help, Lindell kept New York alive to fight another day. With the AL pennant at stake in the last game, the Yankees came out mashing — Jerry Coleman delivered a huge double — and held off a late Boston rally. "Two teams can't win the same pennant," lamented Red Sox Owner Tom Yawkey.

RED SOX–YANKEES

Williams

MUTUAL ADMIRATION SOCIETY

Although it was still several months before the surprise attacks on Pearl Harbor pulled the United States into global conflict, the wider world was already at war on Major League Baseball's Opening Day in 1941. Each game during the season was an escapist moment to savor for a nation under darkening clouds.

Like every aspect of society, the Majors would soon enough be losing some of their top talents to the war effort in the ensuing decade. Prominent among those players who served were the Yankees' Joe DiMaggio and Boston's Ted Williams. Before they swapped their Major League uniforms for military ones, the two rivals produced two of the greatest single-season offensive performances in baseball history.

DiMaggio hit in 56 straight games, a record that remains one of the few seemingly unbreakable benchmarks in sports. Williams, arguably the most gifted hitter of all time, batted .406 on the season. While no one has eclipsed the .400 mark since, the timing proved cruel for the Splendid Splinter, as he would lose the 1941 AL MVP Award to the Yankee Clipper. For all his gifts, Williams couldn't seem to come out on top, finishing second five times, while DiMaggio's Yankees finished the season on the top of the heap a whopping ten times. DiMaggio, because he was a more charismatic figure on the sport's most popular team, received more glory.

Despite the differences in team success, DiMaggio and Williams shared a bond. When they attended a banquet together following their careers, Williams reached for his spectacles and DiMaggio saw a chance for humor. "I never thought you'd need glasses," DiMaggio quipped. Although Williams was not embraced by the press, he never let competition blind him from the magnificence of his rival. Asked about losing MVP honors despite going 6 for 8 on the 1941 season's final afternoon to preserve his historic batting average, Williams repeated, "If I had a vote," he said. "I would've voted for Joe, too."

TALE OF THE TAPE: DiMAGGIO'S AND WILLIAMS' 1941 STATS						
Player	G	R	H	HR	RBI	AVG
DiMaggio	139	122	193	30	125	.357
Williams	143	135	185	37	120	.406

HOME IS WHERE THE HURT IS

Piniella

Before Lou Piniella threw bases at umpires as a manager in Seattle, before he kicked dirt as the home skipper at Wrigley, and before he wrestled with Rob Dibble, his own player, while he was piloting the ballclub in Cincinnati, he was a hot-headed Yankees player. Piniella didn't just play with a single chip on his shoulder; the entire bag was more like it.

Piniella played with fire, a dangerous quality in a combustible rivalry. He ignited what later became known as "The Brawl" with a hard slide into Red Sox catcher Carlton Fisk on May 20, 1976. He was out, erased by right fielder Dwight Evans' perfect throw. No one remembers the result, but rather what followed. The slide was feet-first, but it might as well have been fists-first. The two jumped up and began swinging wildly.

Before it was over, bodies were bruised and Boston pitcher Bill Lee was walking off holding a limp left shoulder after fighting with Mickey Rivers and Graig Nettles. His career was never the same. A Boston reporter wrote, "I went to a baseball game last night and a hockey game broke out."

No quarter is ever given when the Yankees and Red Sox match up, and all actions are endlessly parsed for deeper meanings. Had Piniella slid in hard against the Cleveland Indians, would the result have been different? It's likely.

Thurman Munson and Fisk were at the epicenter of the Yankees–Red Sox rivalry in the 1970s. The All-Star catchers didn't like each other, and the hostility permeated both team's rosters. Munson's disdain stemmed from what he perceived as the media's hype of Fisk. Eventually, the feud became more personal between the two, highlighted by a tussle at home plate after Munson crashed into Fisk in 1973. Piniella provided his bone-crunching sequel three years later.

17

RED SOX–YANKEES

Guidry

BOSTON MASSACRE

Throughout the summer of 1978, the Red Sox thought they were finally exorcising their pinstripe-wearing demons. Instead, it turned out that they were merely delaying their own expiration, making the outcome even more nightmarish.

With the Sox holding a four-game lead over their AL East rivals, the Yankees came to Boston for a four-game weekend series at Fenway in early September. Led by ace Ron Guidry, the Yankees gained control of the AL East with a devastating four-game sweep. Although the romp — dubbed the "Boston Massacre" — only brought the Yankees even with the Red Sox in the standings, it entirely changed the emotional dynamic of the pennant race.

"We felt like they were chasing us now," said Guidry, who won 25 games that season. "The best team we played in those days was the Red Sox. And if you could beat them, you could beat anybody."

The Yankees' series romp that year was payback for 1954, when Boston crushed New York's playoff hopes with a three-game August sweep. But the Yankees never squandered a lead like Boston did in '78.

"All you could do is just sit and wait," recalled Don Zimmer, who managed the Sox during that helpless stretch. "There wasn't much you could do about it. What am I going to do? Bench Carl Yastrzemski or bench Butch Hobson?"

All Boston had to do was achieve mediocrity down the stretch and hope it was enough to stave off New York. But the Sox couldn't recover from the weekend. The final tally from the four-game Boston Massacre: Yankees 42 runs, 67 hits, 4 wins; Boston 9, 21, 0.

"We just couldn't hit when we went into our real bad slump. I had a real good hitting lineup," Zimmer said. "Everybody stopped at one time and we just couldn't score runs."

A NEW VILLAIN

Apprehension had displaced optimism in Kenmore Square by the time the Yankees arrived on Lansdowne Street on Oct. 2, 1978. This was supposed to be the Red Sox's year. They had led the fourth-place Yankees by 14 games in late July. The only thing better than winning the American League East would be embarrassing the Yankees in the process. Not so fast. The Yankees caught the Red Sox in the standings by Sept. 10, and the two clubs finished tied for first place, forcing a one-game cage match for the division crown.

The Yankees loved their chances, running ace Ron Guidry to the mound. He had gone 24-3 on the season and had pitched complete-game shutouts in his previous two outings against Boston. But the day didn't go according to plan, as Guidry was initially outpitched by Boston starter Mike Torrez. The Red Sox led, 2-0, in the seventh inning when the most unlikely hitter dropped a hammer on Boston: Bucky "Bleeping" Dent.

Dent, who managed just five homers on the year, hit a surprising go-ahead, three-run shot over the Green Monster that stunned Boston. Heretofore known only to friends, relatives and the most devoted of Yankees fans, Dent became Boston's most hated villain, which is saying something in a rivalry that also involved Babe Ruth.

Dent is forever remembered for his swing — "A lot of the fans [I see now] were young back then and say, 'Oh, you broke my heart back then,'" Dent recalled. But the game was not decided on his homer, as the Red Sox refused to bow out quietly. With Yankees fireman Goose Gossage on the hill in the ninth inning, Boston got a rally started. With Rick Burleson on first base, Jerry Remy floated a fly ball toward Yankees right fielder Lou Piniella. Piniella lost the ball in the sun, but pretended to camp under it. It dropped at his feet, but Burleson was only able to move up a base. So when Jim Rice followed with a deep fly ball, Burleson could move only to third instead of tagging up and coming home to tie the game. That left Goose versus Carl Yastrzemski with two outs for the AL East crown. Yaz popped out to third base. The Yankees had the victory, and Dent had a new middle name throughout Massachusetts.

SACRIFICIAL JERSEY

The Chicago Cubs, mired in a century of futility in the National League, blame a billy goat and a hex. The Red Sox, meanwhile, blamed the sale of Babe Ruth to the Yankees for their decades-long World Series drought. Over the years, otherwise rational folks in both cities turned to supernatural explanations for the futility of their ballclubs. So who can fault a Red Sox fan for trying to place a curse on the Yankees with a shirt?

During the building of the new Yankee Stadium in 2008, a rogue construction worker buried a replica of Red Sox slugger David Ortiz's jersey at the site in hopes of planting the seeds of some Beantown mojo in the Bronx. While the creative act of "fandalism" curried favor with the citizens of Red Sox Nation, the plan backfired. The jersey became a tabloid sensation, and the Yankees retrieved Big Papi's No. 34 in "an excavation ceremony" two weeks later.

Ortiz, having two reasons not to believe in curses — World Series rings from 2004 and 2007 — dismissed the issue. "I don't pay attention to any of this." Perhaps he had the right idea. Many wondered if the Red Sox fan had gotten it all wrong — that burying such a sacred item actually performed the exact opposite of the intentions by keeping curses away. The Yankees won the World Series in 2009, the club's first season in the new ballpark.

RED SOX–YANKEES

Martinez

DADDY ISSUES

After being acquired from the Montreal Expos in a December 1997 trade, Pedro Martinez turned out to be more than an ace. The Dominican hurler became an icon, inspiring love from Red Sox fans for his performance and willingness to battle the Yankees. Not long after joining the Sox, he said that he wished they could exhume the corpse of Babe Ruth just so he could drill him in the backside. He threw a one-hitter in 1999 with 17 K's, the most ever at Yankee Stadium. He trumped Roger Clemens in the 1999 ALCS, leaving the Fenway Park faithful to chant, "Where is Roger?" In Game 3 of the 2003 ALCS, he nailed Karim Garcia in the back, then pointed at catcher Jorge Posada, seemingly threatening to bean him, too. That led to an ugly exchange between Clemens and Manny Ramirez, and during the ensuing melee, Yankees bench coach Don Zimmer charged Martinez. The pitcher parried his charge like a matador ushering a bull through a red cape. Zim went down hard, and both men came to regret the incident.

The Yankees would get their revenge on Martinez just a few days later in Game 7 of that same series. Having held New York to just two runs through seven frames, Martinez unraveled in the eighth, perhaps a result of being left in a bit too long by Boston skipper Grady Little. The Yankees stormed back to tie the game, setting the stage for another unlikely hero to emerge.

What made this such a delicious matchup is that neither side gave an inch. Including the postseason, Martinez started 39 times against the Yanks, winning 12 and losing 15 with 12 no decisions. He hit 22 batters. After a particularly frustrating regular-season loss to New York in September 2004, Martinez admitted in his post-game comments that he had to call the Yankees "My Daddy." The saying spawned endless chants and a spate of merchandise when the teams tangled in the ALCS just a few weeks later.

Appropriately, Martinez found himself back in the Bronx in the twilight of his career. In 2009, the 38-year-old right-hander started his last games on the World Series stage against the Yankees as a member of the Phillies. Said Martinez, "It doesn't surprise me at all that Boston fans are rooting for me. I know they don't like the Yankees to win, not even in Nintendo games. I am sure that every Boston fan out there can be proud that I am going to beat the Yankees."

RED SOX-YANKEES

Martinez

HEAVYWEIGHT BOUT

Roger Clemens was never afraid to throw inside. He had an unshakable belief in himself and an unwavering focus on helping his team win at any cost. Once viewed as one of the greatest Red Sox pitchers ever, the fireballer who had two 20-K games on his resume and who helped guide the club to the 1986 World Series had become an enemy of Boston by 1999.

After pitching to a lackluster 10-13 record during the 1996 season — the fourth straight campaign in which "The Rocket" had failed to notch a dozen wins — Red Sox General Manager Dan Duquette figured the 13-year veteran was on the downside of his career. Boston let Clemens walk away; a year later, they happily signed his replacement — plucky, 170-pound strikeout artist Pedro Martinez — to a $75-million deal.

One of those personnel moves worked out perfectly.

By 1999, Martinez was a god at Fenway Park, with each of his starts becoming must-see events. Clemens, meanwhile, was a pariah. Not just because he had fizzled out in Boston, but also because he had managed to regain his Cy Young form so quickly after signing with the Toronto Blue Jays in the offseason. Clemens was named the AL's top pitcher in 1997 and '98, but it got even worse for Red Sox Nation in 1999, when he took his inside fastball to another AL East club — the Yankees.

Although the two aces surely weren't in the same weight class, a head-to-head matchup between Pedro and Clemens in Game 3 of the 1999 ALCS was covered like a prize fight. With a raucous Fenway crowd behind him, Martinez leveled his hulking right-handed opponent, working seven innings, allowing just two hits and striking out 12. To the delight of the crowd, Clemens lasted just two innings and was tagged for six hits and five earned runs as Boston rolled to a 13-1 win. John Valentin hit a first-inning home run for the Sox and Boston's tee-off party against Clemens spawned a mocking chant from the Fenway faithful. Their chorus of "Where is Roger?" rang throughout the ballpark after he had been pulled from the game.

TALE OF THE TAPE: CLEMENS AND MARTINEZ										
Player	Team	Years	W-L	ERA	CG	SHO	IP	BB	SO	WHIP
Martinez	Red Sox	1998–2004	117-37	2.52	22	8	1,383.2	309	1,683	0.978
Clemens	Yankees	1999–2003	83-42	4.01	3	2	1,103	398	1,014	1.307

RED SOX-YANKEES

Boone (center)

AARON 'BLEEPING' BOONE

In October 2003, the Red Sox were five outs away from a trip to the World Series, holding a three-run lead in Game 7 of the ALCS with their ace on the hill. All of Red Sox Nation was poised on the edge of ecstasy. What could possibly go wrong?

Try *everything*. Pedro Martinez allowed a double to Yankees shortstop Derek Jeter. Still, no problem, fans thought. Then a single to Bernie Williams. The Sox still led, 5-3. It was going to be fine. Next, Hideki Matsui laced a ground-rule double. Boston Manager Grady Little trotted out to the mound. Seemingly everyone in the ballpark figured Martinez was done. Except for Little, who talked earnestly with Martinez, and walked away *without* his pitcher in tow. There was no second-guessing. It was a first-guessing gasp coming from Boston broadcaster Jerry Remy in the press box. Jorge Posada followed with a double, tying the score. Martinez would say later that Little asked if he had anything left, and he said yes. Little's reasoning was that he wanted his ace to control the outcome. The mistake ultimately cost Little the ALCS and his job — he was replaced by Terry Francona in 2004. It also cost all those fans in Boston the chance to forget yesterday's heartaches.

With the tense matchup moving into the 11th inning tied at five runs apiece, Aaron Boone became the unlikely closer on a Yankees team with Mariano Rivera, who pitched three frames of white-knuckle relief. Mired in a nasty slump — just one extra-base hit in 31 postseason at-bats — Boone didn't even start the game, relegated to the bench behind Enrique Wilson at third. He entered only because the Yankees had burned a pinch-hitter for Wilson in the eighth inning. With the score still tied and knuckleballer Tim Wakefield working his second inning, Boone drilled the first pitch he saw — a hanging knuckleball — into the left-field seats. As he floated around the bases, Boston fans relived a nightmare: Bucky Dent, version 2.0. It was a grand moment for the Yankees' unlikely hero, though. "I just remember telling myself to look and take it all in," Boone said.

RED SOX–YANKEES

Roberts (sliding)

WHEELS OF FIRE

Even in the midst of their title drought, the Red Sox weren't lovable losers. Their close calls were torturous, not slapstick. So when one of their best teams in years stood on the brink of elimination in the 2004 ALCS, it hurt. There the Red Sox were at Fenway Park, after being humiliated by their rivals in three straight games, staring at another painful exit.

Three outs stood between the Red Sox and a broom out of the playoffs. To keep breathing, they would have to rally against the greatest postseason closer ever: the Yankees' Mariano Rivera. Down one run, Kevin Millar walked to lead off the bottom of the ninth. It wasn't much, but it represented a flicker of hope. Dave Roberts entered as a pinch-runner. Acquired from the Dodgers in a relatively nondescript trade deadline move, Roberts was brought to Boston for one purpose: to run.

One of the hardest things to do is steal a base when everyone on both teams knows you're going. After several pick-off attempts, Roberts took off for second. He was safe, barely. He acted like the call wasn't even close the night it happened, but replays showed just how tight the play was. "I hope five or 10 years from now [umpire] Joe West doesn't change his mind," Roberts later joked. Bill Mueller made the swipe matter with a single, as Roberts scored to tie the game.

In the 12th inning, David Oritz, who made the walk-off home run his trademark that year, blasted a towering, game-winning blast. The Red Sox didn't drop another game in the '04 playoffs, ending their 86-year curse with a world title that began with an unlikely comeback in the ALCS — and made Roberts the owner of the most famous stolen base in team history.

THE BLOOD-RED SOCK

For 86 years, there was a fatalist attitude at Fenway Park, summarized thusly: "Only in Boston." Then the Red Sox acquired a pitcher who was summarized thusly, "Only Curt Schilling." Schilling drew the ire of opponents — and occasionally teammates — because of boundless confidence and a vocal personality. Although his opinions could be divisive, Schilling's performance in the clutch was not.

Entering 2004, Schilling was 5-1 in the postseason with a 1.62 ERA. Already a certifiable Yankees killer after his stellar 2001 World Series outings with the Diamondbacks, Schilling left an indelible mark on Red Sox history with his "Bloody Sock" game. Pitching with a torn tendon sheath in his right ankle held together by sutures, he stymied the Yankees through seven innings as blood oozed through his sock in Game 6 of the 2004 ALCS, allowing just one run and setting the stage for an improbable Game 7.

In Game 6, Schilling shared the spotlight with an All-Star nearly as polarizing — Yankees third baseman Alex Rodriguez. Just days after the Bronx Bombers took a commanding 3-games-to-none lead and appeared poised to deliver a knockout blow, they found themselves desperate for a break to keep the Red Sox from forcing a Game 7. With a New York rally brewing in the eighth inning and Bronson Arroyo having replaced Schilling on the hill, Rodriguez hit a slow roller toward first. Arroyo fielded the ball and dashed to tag A-Rod on his way to first. In an attempt to reach first base safely, Rodriguez slapped Arroyo's glove, loosening the ball. He was originally called safe, but it was quickly reversed when umpire Randy Marsh ruled that a player cannot use his arms to commit a malicious act. Rodriguez maintained he did nothing wrong. Of course, Schilling couldn't resist weighing in on the Yankees' questionable play; "That was junior high baseball right there," he said.

SCHILLING'S REGULAR-SEASON BOSTON STATS, 2004-07							
W-L	ERA	G	CG	IP	BB	SO	WHIP
53-29	3.95	119	4	675	108	574	1.215

RED SOX–YANKEES

CURSE REVERSED

It couldn't have happened any other way. Of course the Boston Red Sox would have to reach the promised land by a road no other team had traveled. Never before had a Major League team lost the first three games of a best-of-seven playoff series and won the last four. Yet the Red Sox, having staved off elimination through three nail biters in Games 4, 5 and 6 of the 2004 ALCS, found themselves in a position to accomplish what no one before them ever had, and all of this against their fiercest rivals: the Yankees.

The Sox wasted little time in making sure that Game 7 would be no tight-wire act. They jumped on New York starter Kevin Brown and then pinch-reliever Javier Vazquez, tacking six runs on the board before they'd even made six outs. In all, Boston would score 10 runs, more than enough to back a strong six-inning start from Derek Lowe, to take Game 7 by a 10-3 score, completing a comeback for the ages.

To some, there is nothing supernatural about the game of baseball; it is merely a corporeal competition without divine intervention. Ask a Red Sox fan about the fall of 2004, however, and you may find a large contingent of believers who are assured that something else was at play. From Dave Roberts's steal in Game 4 to David Ortiz's Game 4 and 5 heroics and Johnny Damon's second-inning grand slam in Game 7, all of the big plays the franchise had been missing came at once.

The Red Sox would go on to sweep the St. Louis Cardinals in the World Series, and, suddenly, everything seemed right in New England. The curse of Babe Ruth had been lifted, and a new generation of winning Boston baseball was born.

chapter 2
TRASH TALK

If competition sharpens tongues and familiarity breeds contempt, then it's no wonder that players, managers and franchises that face each other year after year have tossed out some of the sharpest verbal barbs. Whether it's skipper Leo Durocher needling a rival manager or pitcher Curt Schilling making it known that he wasn't afraid of the New York Yankees regardless of what uniform he was wearing, the game's top motor mouths never lacked for confidence. But blabber beware, because although words can be fun and spawn great headlines, they will come back to haunt you if you don't make good on your bold talk.

TALK OF THE TOWN

As a manager, Leo Durocher wanted players with sharp instincts for the game and sharper cleats for takeout slides on the basepaths. He was no less pointed with his words from the dugout, earning the nickname "the Lip." There was no argument that he felt he couldn't win, and no temper tantrum could be too severe. While both worked for the Dodgers, legendary sports broadcaster Red Barber asked Durocher why he couldn't behave like a gentleman. "A nice guy?" Durocher said as he pointed across to the field to the New York Giants' dugout. "Do you know a nicer guy than Mel Ott? Neither does anyone else. All the Giants are nice guys. I don't want to be a nice guy. Nice guys finish last."

That biting proclamation was codified in sporting lore when Durocher took Ott's job in the middle of the 1948 season, shockingly leaving the Dodgers for the Giants. Dodgers fans saw it as an act of treason. The bold move was a year in the making, as Branch Rickey had grown tired of Durocher's act in Brooklyn, both on and off the field. Durocher was suspended for the 1947 season by Commissioner Happy Chandler for "the accumulation of unpleasant incidents."

The Dodgers won the pennant without Durocher in 1947 — Jackie Robinson's first season. The Lip returned the next year but things soured, and he left to manage the crosstown Giants. His quote about Ott, while considered cold-blooded, was validated when he enjoyed his greatest managerial success leading his former rival. He guided the Giants to the 1951 pennant as they erased a 13.5-game deficit and overtook the Dodgers.

Durocher (right)

TRASH TALK

Rollins

TEAMS TO BEAT

Although the New York Mets and Philadelphia Phillies had some brush-ups during their many years in the NL East, it wasn't until both clubs simultaneously fielded talented teams in the 2000s that players in this rivalry began talking more trash than the Sierra Club. In 2006, the Mets rolled to the NLCS, establishing themselves as the division's bullies. Still, Phillies shortstop Jimmy Rollins declared during the ensuing offseason that his club was "the team to beat in the division." When the Phillies stumbled out of the gate, one local paper joked that they were the team to beat and beat and beat.

Rollins' eight-ball prediction still looked misguided as the Phillies trailed the Mets by seven games with 17 to play. Yet Philadelphia went on a tear as the Mets fell into a tailspin. On the season's last day, the Mets were trounced by the Marlins, and Rollins laughed last, going 2 for 3 with a triple and an RBI as the Phillies beat Washington to clinch their first division championship in 14 years.

As the Mets looked to rebound from their '07 swan dive, Carlos Beltran, goaded into responding by the media, touted his Mets as the team to beat in 2008. Prior to Opening Day 2008, Phillies pitcher Cole Hamels countered, labelling the Mets as chokers on a New York radio station.

At the start of the season, the NL East was up for grabs. Although the Mets were tops in the division for much the year, Philadelphia again was the superior team down the stretch as the Mets again missed out on the postseason on the last day of the season. The Phillies remained the team to beat for the next few years, winning the World Series in 2008 over Tampa Bay.

Hamels

TRASH TALK

McGraw

ELEPHANTS IN THE ROOM

While the old myths contend that Abner Doubleday invented the game of baseball, John McGraw might have made a suitable protagonist in that original fable had Doubleday not been available. At the very least, McGraw can take much credit for steering the game's strategy from the Deadball Era and into its modern incarnation.

Having earned the redundant nickname "Little Napoleon" for his stature and his temper, McGraw became arguably the most talented and accomplished Big Leaguer ever to become a manager. The combative McGraw distinguished himself as a skipper by turning the New York Giants into three-time World Series champs. The only thing McGraw liked more than winning was picking fights.

When Connie Mack took charge of the fledgling Philadelphia Athletics in 1901, the same year the American League moved up to Major League status, McGraw laughed the newest competition off as "White Elephants," adding that Mack wouldn't last long in his new job. All Mack did was manage for 50 years, during which time the A's won nine pennants and five World Series. He also defiantly designed the team's elephant insignia — a logo that stuck around as the franchise moved from city to city.

Cone

HIGH SCHOOL BULLY

There's a reason that managers caution their players about stirring the pot. There's always a chance they will end up eating their words. In 1988, New York Mets pitcher David Cone created a controversy by ghost-writing a newspaper column for *The New York Daily News* during the NLCS.

After the Dodgers won Game 1, 3-2, Cone wrote that Los Angeles reliever Jay Howell's curveball was akin to that of a "high school pitcher." The story understandably riled the Dodgers, who then battered Cone for five runs in the first two innings of Game 2, en route to 6-3 victory. On the advice of Mets GM Frank Cashen, Cone stopped writing the piece. Cone apologized to Howell and Dodgers Manager Tommy Lasorda, saying that his attempt at sarcasm missed its mark. Cone scored a measure of redemption in a complete-game Game 6 victory, but Los Angeles wrote the final chapter with a Game 7 triumph, advancing to — and ultimately winning — the World Series.

TRASH TALK

CALLED SHOT

In the years since Babe Ruth revolutionized the game with his powerful swings and epic clouts, Big Leaguers have gone on to hit more home runs in a single season and a career than the Bambino ever did. But no player has ever had the combination of audacity and skill to call his own home run shot in the World Series — and deliver.

Even if it's actually unclear if the Babe really did call that shot, the persistence of the story is a testament to the high regard in which fans hold the Bambino. He's the only player that fans believe would have and could have pulled off the feat.

The Yankees were up, 2 games to none, when the 1932 World Series moved to Wrigley Field for Game 3. Ruth found motivation from more than the stage of the Fall Classic. His friendship with Cubs shortstop Mark Koenig provided fuel. Koenig was a key component on great Yankees teams before being traded to the Cubs in midseason of 1932. Ruth and several of his Yankees teammates were angry after learning that Chicago voted Koenig only a half World Series share, a revenue boon for players when salaries were low. Ruth called the Cubs "cheap." The Cubs called Ruth everything else in the book, riding him about "his increasing weight, racial features … and anything else they could invent," wrote Leigh Montville in his Ruth biography. Ruth was exchanging barbs with the Cubs in the fifth inning when he extended his arm and pointed — that much is clear. Whether Ruth was pointing at the Cubs' bench or pitcher Charlie Root or the outfield seats is uncertain. What he did next is not: Ruth blasted a home run to center field and trotted around the bases letting the Cubs hear all about it.

Ruth

TRASH TALK

McGraw

THE LAST WORD

The lasting image of reliever Tug McGraw is jubilant, if not narrow. When he recorded the final out of the 1980 World Series for the Phillies, the long-haired, zany reliever raised his arms in triumph. It was vindication for a pitcher, and celebration for a city. Despite having baseball in town since the founding of the National League, this was Philadelphia's first-ever World Series title.

McGraw, as a result, is often remembered by fans as a Phillie. But he was also pretty special as a Met. Both franchises take some ownership of him, likely because McGraw is considered one of the game's greatest personalities. He punctuated final outs with hard slaps of his glove onto his thigh. His long hair attracted as much attention as his quotes. But at the Phillies' victory parade in 1980, McGraw outdid himself. He told New York City: "Take this championship and shove it." Those in attendance said it was the loudest roar that they had ever heard from a Philadelphia crowd.

McGraw never shied away from controversy, but he was still an unlikely instigator. After all, McGraw made his name and won a World Series with the Mets, pitching for the "miracle" team in 1969. The left-hander also coined the Mets' 1973 slogan: "Ya Gotta Believe." Yet McGraw didn't forget when the Mets let him walk after the 1974 season. The New York brass thought he was damaged goods because of a torn shoulder muscle. McGraw went on to pitch for the Phillies from 1975–84. He became a star, appearing everywhere on TV and radio. His nickname was easy for fans to remember and his looks made him easy to recognize. But in Philadelphia, he will always be remembered for the last word on the city's first World Series championship.

McGRAW'S STATS WITH THE METS AND PHILLIES							
Team	W-L	ERA	G	SV	IP	SO	WHIP
Phillies	49-37	3.10	463	94	722	491	1.198
Mets	47-55	3.17	361	86	792.2	618	1.306

TRASH TALK

CHATTERBOX

Curt Schilling has never had an opinion he wouldn't share. He likes to weigh in on all topics, seemingly feeling like an issue can't be resolved until he discusses it. This comfort in the spotlight rubbed some opponents the wrong way, until, of course, they realized they'd much rather hear him talk than face him on the mound.

Schilling's reputation for postseason verbosity began in earnest in 2001 when he was the twin-ace of the Diamondbacks, along with left-hander Randy Johnson. After leading the Majors in wins during the regular season, Schilling was dominant as Arizona navigated the NL playoffs. When asked during the World Series about the "mystique and aura" of the Yankees, he chided, "Those are dancers in a nightclub."

The D-backs won that '01 Series with a dramatic, walk-off bloop hit by Luis Gonzalez in Game 7, and Schilling backed up his words by allowing a paltry four runs through 21.1 innings of work. After being traded to Boston in 2004, his "Bloody Sock" victory over the New York Yankees in the '04 ALCS only cemented his legend. Said Schilling shortly before that game at Yankee Stadium, "I'm not sure I can think of any scenario more enjoyable than making 55,000 people from New York shut up."

After helping lead the Red Sox to an historic comeback in the 2004 ALCS and eventually to their first World Series title since 1918, he said dismissively of the Yankees, "I was front row and center when their quote-unquote dynasty ended."

SCHILLING'S CAREER POSTSEASON STATS							
W-L	ERA	G	CG	IP	BB	SO	WHIP
11-2	2.23	19	4	133.1	25	120	0.968

Terry

REACTIONARIES

The Brooklyn Dodgers, affectionately known as "Dem Bums" after years of also-ran finishes, didn't like the New York Giants. For their part, the Giants certainly didn't like the Dodgers. They ribbed each other whenever possible. In the winter of 1934, the Dodgers were a bit of a mess. They were looking for new leadership. The front office summoned Casey Stengel from California for an interview. He had been working in the Minor Leagues and was relatively unknown. The Dodgers took a chance and hired Stengel, but not before agreeing to pay the manager he replaced — Max Carey — his salary for the season to do nothing.

Such business practices weren't going to escape the Giants' silver tongues. As the Dodgers underwent their awkward turnover, Giants Manager Bill Terry remarked, "Is Brooklyn still in the league?" It was a great line, but would prove the pitfalls of trash talking. As the Giants were trying to secure the pennant seven months later, the Dodgers stood in their way. They were still mad, providing motivation for a team that wasn't in the hunt. Playing in front of loud, passionate home fans, Stengel's Dodgers beat the Giants twice in the season's last two days. Those wins gift-wrapped the pennant for St. Louis and effectively jammed Terry's words down his throat.

chapter 3
CUBS-CARDINALS

The uneasy relationship between the St. Louis Cardinals and Chicago Cubs owes more to geography than head-to-head combat, but is no less fierce for that distinction. Compared to the bustle and sprawl of Chicago, St. Louis might seem an overmatched foe, but when it comes to baseball the Redbirds have been the powerhouse. For its part, the city of Chicago was able to nab beloved broadcaster Harry Caray from St. Louis, and the city's legion of devoted fans has also been blessed with the "Friendly Confines" of Wrigley Field, one of the most idyllic places to take in a ballgame on a summer day. For a time, Wrigley was also home to the game's sunniest superstar in Ernie Banks. While Banks and Caray brought a joie de vivre to Wrigley, the festivities during their tenures never involved a World Series triumph, which has become a common cause for celebration in St. Louis.

THE VOICE

Before idiosyncratic and enthusiastic broadcaster Harry Caray became a bespectacled nationwide folk hero calling games for the Chicago Cubs, before he turned "Take Me Out to the Ball Game" during the seventh-inning stretch at Wrigley Field into an event bigger than the ball game itself, Harry Christopher Carabina was a St. Louis man. His trademark excitable style added spice to Cardinals broadcasts that, even he admitted, were previously as "boring as crop reports." Yet the Cards let him go in 1969.

A stopover in the Oakland Athletics' broadcast booth was followed by an 11-year run with the White Sox at Comiskey Park. In 1982, he moved across town to the Cubs' booth. Some die-hard Cardinals and Sox fans had trouble seeing — and hearing — Caray as Mr. Cub, but it was clear that he was a perfect fit. Caray's wide regional appeal became national thanks to WGN's growing television audience. Before long, Caray was the de facto eyes and ears for baseball fans in many television markets that didn't have Big League teams. Calling games for Cubbie teams that struggled through most of the 1980s and '90s, Caray eventually became more of a celebrity than even some of the team's players. He became the face of the franchise and entertained many guests at Wrigley. In the hallway behind his former booth at Wrigley Field, there's a picture of Caray broadcasting with President Ronald Reagan.

"The Cubs fans loved him, the White Sox fans loved him, the Cardinals fans loved him," said Cardinals' Hall of Famer Stan Musial. "He was always the life of the party, the life of baseball."

CUBS-CARDINALS

Brock

STEAL OF A DEAL

When the Cardinals acquired fleet-footed right fielder Lou Brock in 1964, it seemed like a steal — for the Cubs. The Chicago front office had grown impatient with the skinny kid from Arkansas, whose average wasn't strong enough to hold down the leadoff spot. Mindful of the axiom that you can't steal first base, the Cubs jumped at the opportunity to swap Brock for Cardinals pitchers Ernie Broglio and Bobby Shantz as part of a six-player deal. Broglio had won 27 games as a starter the previous two seasons, and although he just had three victories at the time of the midseason trade in '64, he brought a proven arm to the Cubs' rotation — at least that's what the Cubs thought. But it turned out Broglio was hurt, and he won just seven games for Chicago over the next three years.

"I don't want to cast any shadows on the deal," said Broglio. "But the Cardinals knew that I had a bad arm when they made the deal. I had bad feelings about it, especially after they won [the 1964 World Series]."

Maligned as a one-tool player in Chicago, Brock found comfort in St. Louis. He was told by management to roam the outfield and run aggressively to stretch singles into doubles and two-base hits into triples. He developed into a solid offensive player and in 1979, at the age of 40, became the 14th man to reach 3,000 hits. He also stole a record 938 career bases, including 118 in a single season, but these marks were later broken by Rickey Henderson. Still, not bad for a guy whose first club was happy to unload him. As he reached 3,000 hits, *The Chicago Tribune* called the 1964 deal "the biggest robbery since Brinks."

CUBS-CARDINALS

Sandberg

THE SANDBERG GAME

The 1984 season seemed promising at Wrigley Field after the Cubs posted a 12-8 April record, tying them for first place entering May. But the '84 campaign didn't officially become one to savor until June 23, when the feel-good stretch became something even more significant. The Cubs were already five games above .500 and were 1.5 games behind in the division when the Cardinals came to town for a nationally televised game.

The Cubs trailed in a wild one, 9-8, when second baseman Ryne Sandberg stepped to the plate in the ninth inning against former Cub and future Hall of Famer Bruce Sutter. Sandberg was just a kid, and even though he was 3 for 4 on the day, nobody expected him to do much against Sutter. Yet the 24-year-old defied the odds, hitting just the fourth homer that Sutter had relinquished all year to tie the game. After a two-run 10th by the Cardinals put them ahead, up stepped Sandberg again. He proceeded to hit his second logic-defying home run off Sutter, this one tying the game. The Cubs eventually won on Dave Owen's pinch-hit single in the 11th, but the day was forever remembered in Chicago as Sandberg's coming out party, pushing the Cubs toward the playoffs for the first time in 39 years.

"He's Baby Ruth," Cardinals Manager Whitey Herzog joked with reporters after Sandberg's 5-for-6, seven-RBI breakout. "He's the greatest player ever."

Sandberg was voted the National League MVP that season, en route to forging a Hall of Fame career of his own. In the ensuing years, Sandberg had trouble wrapping his head around what transpired on that defining day against the Cubs' archrival.

"I was almost in a fog after the game," Sandberg told *The Chicago Tribune*. "That game really propelled the team."

Alexander

OLD PETE

In 1926, Grover "Pete" Alexander was entering his ninth season with the Cubs — and 16th overall. The 39-year-old was causing his club a lot of headaches, the most recent being an indefinite suspension for showing up to batting practice before a game in Philadelphia under the influence of alcohol. Alexander drank heavily because he believed it controlled his epilepsy.

Cubs President Bill Veeck had grown tired of Alexander's ornery act and placed him on waivers on June 22, 1926, where he was quickly snagged by the Cardinals for the price of $4,000.

The Cubs had little reason to think they would regret the deal. Then, Alexander delivered a career-defining moment in Game 7 of the World Series with the Cardinals facing a stacked Yankees club featuring Babe Ruth and Lou Gehrig. St. Louis led, 3-2, in the seventh inning, when Alexander was awoken from a nap in the bullpen. He came in and shut down the Yankees the rest of the way, earning St. Louis a world championship and the Cubs a punch in the gut.

CUBS-CARDINALS

LEADING THE CHARGE

Dusty Baker was a part-time player for the Oakland Athletics in 1986 when 41-year-old Tony La Russa was named manager of the A's during the season. He was the third to take the reins during a tumultuous season. After that '86 campaign, the 37-year-old Baker retired — soon to embark on a managerial career of his own. The pair clearly never became friendly while briefly sharing a dugout.

It's unclear if the Baker-La Russa feud grew roots in Oakland, but it was in full bloom by the time they took over the Cubs and Cardinals, respectively. As manager of the Giants, Baker objected to La Russa's tactic of "baiting" Barry Bonds into expanding his strike zone prior to the 2002 NLCS. Both were fined after Game 1 of that series for failing to aid the umpires in restoring order when the benches cleared during the game.

In 2003, Baker was named skipper of the Cubs, and his running battle with La Russa resumed in the cauldron of one of baseball's fiercest rivalries. The vitriol spilled over to the players and a beanball war ensued in September 2003. Ugly words led to a pregame meeting on the field between the simmering skippers, prompting Baker to say afterwards, "There was nothing to laugh about."

While the two were helming the opposing sides of the rivalry, Baker's Cubs held a slim edge, 37 wins to 34 for the Cardinals, during the regular season. Although his teams were some of the Cubs' most competitive in years — coming within just five outs of the pennant in 2003 — they would not match the postseason success of La Russa and the Cards, who won the 2006 World Series.

Even after Baker moved to another gig, these two kept at it. In August 2010, Baker's Cincinnati Reds became embroiled in a brouhaha with the Cardinals.

"Like I say, there are times that you beat us — if we're not good enough — but you're never going to scare us, and we're never going to back down," La Russa said.

Baker (left), La Russa

BY THE NUMBERS: LA RUSSA'S CARDINALS AND BAKER'S CUBS FROM 2003-06				
Team	W-L	NL Central titles	NL pennants	World Series titles
Cardinals	373-274	3	2	1
Cubs	322-326	1	0	0

CUBS-CARDINALS

Cardwell (top row, fourth from right)

NO FLY ZONE

On May 13, 1960, young right-handed pitcher Don Cardwell was traded from the Phillies to the Cubs. It didn't seem like a significant move at the time — Cardwell was sporting a 1-2 record and 4.45 ERA — but it was a deal that left its mark on the Cardinals–Cubs rivalry and baseball history. All it took was two days for Cardwell to make 33,500 new fans at Wrigley Field. On May 15, in his first start with the Cubs, Cardwell threw a no-hitter against the Cardinals, striking out seven and walking just one while retiring the last 26 hitters he faced.

The only no-no in the history of this rivalry could not have happened without some stellar defense, including a catch by left fielder Walt "Moose" Moryn to end the game and preserve history. Cardwell's no-hitter remains the only one of its kind: a no-no thrown in a player's first start with a team. Cardwell would go on to pitch for the Cubs for two more seasons with a 30-44 record and 4.31 ERA, but he'll be most remembered for that spring day in the friendly confines.

WELL SUITED

There are times that the Cubs–Cardinals conflict doesn't make a lot of sense. The idea was to beat one another, right? Yet on at least three occasions, the Cubs traded Hall-of-Fame players to their archrivals. Sixteen years after dealing Lou Brock to Chicago, the Cubs shipped closer Bruce Sutter, one of the game's most dominant relief pitchers, to St. Louis.

At the time, the rationale seemed sound: The Cubs didn't think they had a chance to contend, even with Sutter anchoring their bullpen. So they peddled him to St. Louis for multiple players, including slugging first baseman Leon Durham and third baseman Ken Reitz.

"With Sutter, the [Cardinals] can win the pennant," Cubs General Manager Bob Kennedy said. "With Sutter alone we don't think we can win the pennant. We are in a rebuilding program."

What was left unsaid was that Sutter was making $700,000 in the final year of his contract after winning an arbitration case that many around the Majors viewed as fiscal Armageddon, because it pointed toward seven-figure salaries. Armed with his revolutionary split-finger fastball, Sutter left the Cubs shaking their heads in disgust again. He saved 127 games for the Cardinals over four seasons, in addition to being their stopper in 1982 when they won the World Series.

Sutter

SUTTER'S STATS WITH CARDINALS AND CUBS								
Team	W-L	ERA	GF	SV	IP	BB	SO	WHIP
Cardinals	26-30	2.72	203	127	396.2	111	259	1.165
Cubs	32-30	2.39	222	133	493	149	494	1.055

CUBS-CARDINALS

Lee

TWO FOR THREE

No Major Leaguer had swapped his helmet for a Triple Crown since 1967. Not since Red Sox masher Carl Yastrzemski led the AL with a .326 average, 44 homers and 121 RBI had anyone claimed a league's top spot in each of the game's three most prominent offensive stats. A pair of dueling NL Central first basemen looked to end that in 2005.

Chicago's 29-year-old Derrek Lee and St. Louis's 25-year-old rising megastar Albert Pujols reduced the longstanding tussle between the two franchises down to a mano-a-mano battle between two scorching hitters. Both pushed Yaz's hold on the title of "Last Remaining Triple Crown Winner" to the test as they battled atop the NL leaderboards. Entering a four-game series against one another in mid-September — one that carried little relevance in the standings — Lee had the edge on Pujols in homers (by three) and average (by .004), while Pujols held to a rather comfortable nine-RBI lead. Neither player would budge; Pujols ended up leading the NL in RBI with 117, Lee in average with a .335 mark and Atlanta's Andruw Jones in homers with 51.

Lee would finish his stellar 2005 campaign by adding 46 homers and 107 RBI. Pujols, for his part, finished with a .330 batting average and 41 homers.

Pujols

CUBS-CARDINALS

Sosa (left), McGwire

BLAST OFF

According to the pop music charts, the soundtrack to the summer and fall of 1998 may have been Aerosmith's "I Don't Want to Miss a Thing," but the sound ringing in the ears of baseball fans was that of bats cracking baseballs, as homers were flying out of Big League ballparks at a record pace. Leading the barrage were Cardinals first baseman Mark McGwire and Cubs right fielder Sammy Sosa.

For the better part of summer and fall, the lead story in sports pages was the pair's assault on one of the game's most hallowed marks — Roger Maris's single-season home run record of 61. An older generation of baseball fans was transported back to that memorable '61 season, when Maris and his teammate Mickey Mantle both chased Babe Ruth's record.

McGwire's and Sosa's highlights and box scores were followed closely. Their press conferences became must-see events, intertwining the rival franchises with games that became "revival meetings." McGwire was a shy man, leaving Sosa to provide flavor and a smile to their pursuit of history. McGwire may have had a slight advantage by being on a team that wasn't going to the playoffs, affording him the luxury of focusing solely on the homer race, while Sosa was a catalyst for a playoff-bound club. After a 20-home run June, Sosa seemingly had the better shot to eclipse the single-season home run record. But Big Mac had saved an amazing closing burst for the final leg of the season, swatting five home runs in his last 19 swings. He finished with 70, a mark that would only stand until 2001. Sosa topped out at 66.

"To hit 70 balls out in batting practice isn't too easy for many people," said Expos Manager Felipe Alou, who felt that Sosa's accomplishment was being overlooked.

Said McGwire, "I can't believe I did it. Can you? It absolutely blows me away."

Mays

chapter 4
MAN TO MAN

Baseball is a team game, at least by definition, but the sport is comprised of solo confrontations measuring one player's strength against another. Those matchups sometimes come in the form of a thrilling hitter-pitcher battle, with a man on the mound staring down his bat-wielding opponent. Other times, it's managers matching wits. Individual rivalries emerge when players are constantly vying for a pennant or a World Series title. They are amplified when players are pursuing greatness at the cost of their peers, like an all-time strikeout record or home run crown. When these matchups repeat themselves time and again with everything on the line, the business of winning baseball games will almost inevitably turn personal.

KINGS OF NEW YORK

Willie Mays, Mickey Mantle, Duke Snider — their names are enough to turn an older generation of fans into little kids again, and to have them romanticizing about black-and-white highlights and childish nicknames. Baseball essentially had the sports page to itself throughout the 1950s, with three of the game's greatest players taking center stage and patrolling center field for three New York rivals, creating an argument that still percolates today; who was better: Willie, Mickey or the Duke?

Judging by statistics alone, Mays, the Giants' five-tool star, was the top talent. Playing home games in the spacious Polo Grounds and later at Candlestick Park, Mays hit .302 with 660 home runs over 22 seasons. He was the most well-rounded player of his era, not sacrificing speed for power. A breathtaking defensive player, Mays' catch in Game 1 of the 1954 World Series remains one of most iconic in the game's history.

Mantle batted .298 with 536 career homers while appearing in a dozen World Series for the Yankees, despite having his career undermined by injuries. "The Mick" was arguably the best switch-hitter ever to play in the Majors. Mantle won seven Series, including one against the "Say Hey Kid" in 1951. Had injuries not hampered him, his production could have rivaled Mays'.

"The Duke of Flatbush" joined the pair in Cooperstown by hitting .295 with 407 home runs. A mighty left-handed slugger, Snider hit more home runs than any other Major Leaguer during the 1950s. He's immortalized in Roger Kahn's *Boys of Summer* for bringing the Brooklyn Dodgers — "Dem Bums" — their lone World Series championship in 1955. The Dodgers' title was part of a glorious stretch that featured Mays, Snider and Mantle each winning titles over a three-year run.

"They used to run a box in the New York papers comparing me to Mickey Mantle and Willie Mays," Snider said. "It was a great time for baseball."

Said Commissioner Bowie Kuhn, "It was one of the rare times that Casey Stengel was laconic when he was asked who was better of the center fielders. His answer was he would take all three of them."

MAN TO MAN

Brett (restrained)

| BRETT'S CAREER STATS VS. GOSSAGE ||||||||||| |
AB	H	2B	HR	RBI	BB	SO	AVG	OBP	SLG	OPS
38	11	2	3	11	5	2	.289	.364	.579	.943

A ROYAL PAIN

Repeated, riveting playoff confrontations throughout the 1970s made rivals out of a California kid named George Brett and a human No. 2 pencil from Colorado Springs known as Goose Gossage. The Royals' slugging third baseman and the Yankees' flamethrowing reliever were at the center of the heated Kansas City–New York battles for the American League pennant and, of course, the "Pine Tar" Incident.

History says that Gossage, a Hall of Famer, was one of the fiercest closers ever. He averaged nearly a strikeout per inning in his first 11 years on the job. While Gossage recorded the final out to clinch a division, league or World Series seven times, he had all kinds of trouble retiring Brett. The Royals' Hall of Fame third baseman was a three-time batting champ and went 11 for 38 against Gossage with three home runs in his career.

The first player enshrined in Cooperstown sporting a Royals cap, Brett hit a dramatic home run off Gossage in Game 3 of the 1980 American League Championship Series. Yet the pair's most memorable confrontation occurred on July 24, 1983. By then, the teams had faced off in the ALCS in four of the previous seven years. And like so many times during those classic battles, Brett turned on a Gossage heater, this time for a go-ahead, two-run home run. But the Yankees, thanks to the eagle eyes of skipper Billy Martin, appealed to the umpire to enforce a little-known rule regarding pine tar extending beyond 18 inches from the tip of the bat. Brett was ruled out, and he blew his top, charging out of the dugout to argue with home plate umpire Tim McClelland. After the game, Kansas City formally protested McClelland's decision — successfully, as it turned out — and won when the game was resumed three weeks later. The incident forged a bond between Brett and Gossage and years away from the game cooled their volcanic rivalry.

"I'm sure George will give me credit for making him famous," Gossage joked. "But I've got to say that he's the greatest hitter I have ever faced."

SMOKING CANNON

Negro Leagues players were proving their talent long before Jackie Robinson broke the Major League color barrier in 1947 with the Brooklyn Dodgers. Among the star players gathering attention on both sides of the sport's color line before Robinson came along was Satchel Paige, who some claimed was the best pitcher who ever lived. But the loquacious Paige insisted that there had been Negro Leagues aces whose prodigious talents equalled his own.

At the turn of the century, hurlers Smokey Joe Williams and Dick "Cannonball" Redding provided the footprints for Paige to follow. They were the Nolan Ryan and Randy Johnson of the Negro Leagues as they dominated and amazed opponents on barnstorming tours. Their nicknames were traced to their fastballs, believed to be among the best ever. Both were posthumously elected to Cooperstown.

At 6 foot 4, 200 pounds, the Texas-born Williams was a big man even by today's standards. Although he played with eight different clubs, he is best remembered as a fireballer for the Homestead Grays. But his performance level rarely dipped below superb regardless of his jersey. In 1914, he went 41-3, and he also compiled a 20-7 record against white teams in exhibition games. He twice outdueled Walter Johnson, according to records kept by the Negro League Baseball Players Association. He once struck out 27 batters in a game at age 44, making him an ageless wonder decades before Ryan.

Redding starred for nearly three decades, beginning in 1911. At the age of 21, he went 43-12 with six no-hitters and a perfect game. Ty Cobb, who was generally loath to issue compliments, said that Redding would have been a 30-game winner in the Big Leagues. Cobb thought so much of Redding's talent that he refused to take batting practice against the right-hander who, legend has it, fanned Babe Ruth three times on nine pitches.

Williams

MAN TO MAN

Lasorda

Phanatic

TOMMY LASORDA VS. THE PHILLIE PHANATIC

Los Angeles Dodgers skipper Tommy Lasorda had a history of being a willing foil for the Phillie Phanatic when he would bring his ballclub to Philadelphia's Veterans Stadium, but 1988 saw his taste for the mascot go from good humor to *Goodfellas*.

During an August game, the sideshow turned ugly after Lasorda took offense with the Phanatic's routine in front of the Dodgers' dugout. Lasorda lost his cool when the mascot mocked the rotund Lasorda's role as a pitchman for a weight-loss drink and then dragged a dummy wearing a Dodgers uniform onto the field.

"If he wants to entertain, he wants to dance, wants to carry kids around the field, that's great," Lasorda said. "But I don't believe in demonstrating violence at the ballpark. And that's what he does with the dummy."

The Phanatic, no dummy himself, tried to make peace with Lasorda when he entered the field for his last skit of the day. The dummy was still in tow, but The Beatles' "I Want to Hold Your Hand" played over the P.A. system as the mascot tried to make amends with the scorned skipper.

Paige (left), Dean

FRIENDLY FIRE

Satchel Paige and Dizzy Dean both had a unique way with words and pitches. At the end of his lengthy playing career, which included time in both the Negro Leagues and the Majors, Paige handed autograph-seekers a business card that listed his staple tips for living a long and healthy life, including the value of not running, of avoiding fried meat and of never looking back "because something might be gaining on you."

Dean and Paige were two of a kind, yet remained solo acts in separate leagues due to segregation. Both were showmen, though, who used their talent to entertain and both used barnstorming tours to supplement their income. When the two paired off in a 1934 exhibition game, it was an epic matchup, the first of several the two engineered. When they faced off, they liked to mimic each other's styles to amuse the fans. Using pitches like the "hurry up" and "bat dodger," Paige drove his collection of all-stars to a 1-0 victory in 13 innings. In that first meeting, Paige struck out 17 while Dean fanned 15. Along the way, Paige gained the respect of Dean, one of the Big Leagues' top aces at the time.

"Let 'em argue. The best pitcher I've seen is ol' Satchel Paige," Dean said. "My fastball looks like a change of pace alongside that li'l pistol bullet Satch shoots up the plate."

Indians Owner Bill Veeck signed Paige 14 years later to reinforce his bullpen during the 1948 pennant race. The image of Paige's 1934 clash with Dean remained imprinted on his brain.

"It was the best I've ever seen," Veeck said. For his part, Paige admitted that Dean had a "fastball in his class."

Dean and Paige continued to stage exhibition games even after Dean retired to the broadcast booth, paving the way to help break baseball's color barrier. Dean claimed that he made more money when he wasn't in a Big League uniform than when he was in it, especially when the star opposing attraction was his buddy Paige.

MAN TO MAN

DiMaggio

TRADING PLACES

Williams

If baseball ever created its own version of Mount Rushmore, then the faces of Yankees icon Joe DiMaggio and Red Sox hero Ted Williams would likely be on it. Both were supremely gifted hitters throughout their careers, but the numbers each posted during their 1941 season battle, which remains one of the most remarkable duels ever, might just have been enough to get them sculpted in that mountainside. DiMaggio compiled a 56-game hitting streak while Williams finished the season with a .406 batting average. Neither mark has been equalled since.

In 1949, they were nearly traded for each other. The story goes that Red Sox Owner Tom Yawkey and Yankees co-owner Dan Topping started talking trade on a train to baseball's annual owners' meetings. Over drinks, the conversation switched from finances to the team's rosters. Topping explained that the Yankees really needed a left-handed slugger in their lineup to take advantage of the short right-field porch in the Bronx. And it just so happened that the Red Sox were seeking a right-handed hitter who could play ping-pong off the Green Monster. The left-handed Williams for the right-handed DiMaggio, straight-up?

It almost made too much sense. Yawkey and Topping supposedly wrapped a long night of partying by shaking on the deal. When the owners awoke the next morning, sobriety and reality intervened. Both wanted to make sure the other was joking; that they couldn't possibly exchange the two symbols of their franchises.

Former Yankees Manager Casey Stengel helped leak the gossip, admitting that such a conversation had taken place, though he tried to downplay it. Had such talk occurred today, it would make the Internet instantaneously combust. In the end, the idea was shelved, and DiMaggio and Williams both went to the Hall of Fame, having battled for championships and accolades for decades as lifelong members of their respective sides in the Yankees–Red Sox rivalry.

MAN TO MAN

Wood

Johnson

FLAME WARS

By 1912, the Washington Senators' 24-year-old Walter Johnson was already a bona fide ace. His fastball had earned him the nickname "The Big Train" and helped him top 300 strikeouts in 1910. During the 1912 campaign, he reeled off 16 straight wins to set a new AL record, only to have young Boston Red Sox fireballer "Smoky" Joe Wood come charging after him to equal the mark.

"Can I throw harder than Joe Wood? Listen, there's no man alive that can throw harder than Smoky Joe Wood," the affable Johnson said.

On Sept. 6, 1912, the two faced off at Fenway Park. Johnson's streak of wins had recently ended at 16, but Washington Manager Clark Griffith still convinced Red Sox skipper Jake Stahl to juggle his rotation so Johnson could defend his record against Wood, who had won 13 straight.

Naturally, the two engaged in a pitchers' duel, stringing together enough zeroes for a lottery jackpot. In the sixth inning, Senators outfielder Danny Moeller was unable to snag a pop fly, allowing the Red Sox to score the game's only run. The outfielder was despondent afterward, leaving Johnson to console him. "Don't feel badly. I should have struck [the hitter] out."

Wood's excellence was accomplished without the use of a spitter, a common weapon during that era. The 22-year-old finished the season 34-5 with a 1.91 ERA, but conceded that Johnson was the "greatest pitcher who ever lived."

Despite getting the best of Johnson on that day, Wood could not match his foe's consistency. He went 11-5 in 1913, while Johnson recorded 36 wins with a minuscule 1.14 ERA on his express path to Cooperstown.

TALE OF THE TAPE: JOHNSON'S AND WOOD'S STATS IN 1912									
Player	W-L	ERA	CG	SHO	SV	IP	BB	SO	WHIP
Wood	34-5	1.91	35	10	1	344	82	258	1.015
Johnson	33-12	1.39	34	7	2	369	76	303	0.908

MAN TO MAN

Paige (left), Gibson

THE POWER AND THE FURY

A born showman, there was no crowd that Satchel Paige couldn't have eating out of his hand, no pitcher he couldn't outduel, and no batter he wouldn't try to intimidate. On the mound, he had few equals. Off the mound, he had none. That made his showdowns with Negro Leagues slugger Josh Gibson all the more appealing. Gibson, a legend in his own right, was coined the "Brown Bambino" for prodigious home runs that flew as high and far as any hit by Babe Ruth.

Although they were opponents in the Negro Leagues, the Paige-Gibson rivalry was different because they were quite frequently teammates on barnstorming tours across the country, playing against well-known Major Leaguers. Those moonlighting gigs were part of their personal race to get signed when the sport finally integrated.

Their most memorable confrontation came on July 21, 1942, during the Negro Leagues World Series in Pittsburgh. Paige's Kansas City Monarchs led, 4-0, against Gibson's favored Homestead Grays. The high-profile event was an ideal stage for Paige's Vaudeville act on the mound. After telling Monarchs first baseman Buck O'Neil of his plan, he intentionally walked a pair of hitters to bring Gibson to the plate.

While this sort of maneuver likely infuriated his manager, it delighted the crowd. With Gibson at the dish, Paige then announced his pitches before throwing them, frustrating the hulking slugger. Three fastballs, three strikes, and Gibson was out, leaving Paige to walk off the mound in triumph.

Gibson was the Paul Bunyan of the Negro Leagues. Legend has it that he hit the only fair ball that entirely left Yankee Stadium. In one exhibition game, Cardinals ace Dizzy Dean stationed his center fielder, Jimmy Ripple, 450 feet from the plate, and to the crowd's amazement, Gibson flied out to that very spot.

Paige would later describe Gibson as "the greatest hitter who ever lived." Paige ultimately reached the Big Leagues as a 40-something rookie, but Gibson died of a stroke before ever getting the opportunity to play in the integrated Major Leagues.

MAN TO MAN

Robinson (left), McGraw

A FALLING OUT

With friends like John McGraw, Wilbert Robinson hardly needed enemies. As players, McGraw and Robinson were critical components of the bare-knuckle Baltimore Orioles in the 1890s. McGraw carried that same tenacity with him as a manager, where he turned the New York Giants into a powerhouse. He groomed Robinson as a coach and then, just as quickly, turned on him. McGraw belittled Robinson in 1916 after Robinson's Brooklyn club defeated the Giants for the pennant. McGraw claimed the Dodgers only beat his Giants because his team tanked the games. The insinuation understandably infuriated Robinson.

"He couldn't stand to lose and deserted his team," Robinson fired back. "McGraw and I have been in baseball for 30 years. During that time we have played innumerable games and I defy McGraw to show me one of those that was not won on its merits."

TEXAS TOAST

Nolan Ryan threw seven no-hitters during his decorated Big League pitching career. But a generation of fans too young to watch him dominate in the 1970s and '80s with the Astros and Angels remembers him best for six *punches* he threw for the Texas Rangers on Aug. 4, 1993, at Arlington Stadium.

In the top of the third inning of a game the Rangers trailed, 2-0, Ryan grazed the White Sox's Robin Ventura with a pitch. Ventura, who was known for his clubhouse leadership, started to walk to first, then changed his mind. He bolted toward the 46-year-old Ryan. Just as quickly, Ryan wrapped Ventura in a headlock, resembling a rodeo cowboy bringing down a steer. The White Sox's leader took six socks to the noggin before the mound became a moshpit of players from both sides.

Baseball lifers were shocked that Ventura had the audacity to charge the venerable Ryan, the all-time leader in strikeouts. Cleveland skipper Mike Hargrove said that "going after Nolan is like going after the Lincoln Memorial." Columnists generally took Ryan's side, praising his knockout of the younger Ventura as inspiration for middle-aged men everywhere.

The White Sox and other opponents who had tired of Ryan's tower-buzzing pitches were more sympathetic to Ventura. Said Angels Manager Buck Rodgers, "Nolan Ryan is no angel. It's pride and you've got to do something."

When the Rangers advanced to their first World Series in the fall of 2010, the clip of Ryan clobbering Ventura ran on the JumboTron, hyping up fans before the first pitch.

MAN TO MAN

Jackson

Martin

A STIRRING DEBATE

Billy Martin and Reggie Jackson were never a great fit. Martin was a sleeves-rolled-up grinder who fought for everything. Jackson was a supremely talented superstar thought to have an ego perfect for the Big Apple. Shortly after Jackson joined the Yankees for the 1977 season, Martin asserted his authority, batting the slugger fifth instead of slotting him into his customary cleanup spot.

Martin wanted no-nonsense players in the mold of Yankees captain Thurman Munson, who didn't like the new hotshot either. The clubhouse tension reached a boiling point when Jackson told *Sport* magazine, "I'm the straw that stirs the drink. Munson thinks he can stir the drink but he can only stir it bad."

On June 18, during a nationally televised game at Fenway Park, Martin felt Jackson loafed after Jim Rice's flyball to right field and pulled him from the game right then and there. Screaming "I have had enough of his stuff," the volcanic Martin sent Paul Blair in as Jackson's replacement. Jackson threw his arms up in disbelief, jogged in from the outfield and immediately exchanged words with his skipper. The dispute escalated in the dugout, with Martin suggesting that it was time that he beat up the much younger and stronger Jackson. Jackson replied, "Who do you think you are talking to, old man?" And just like that, the brawl was on. Yankees coaches Yogi Berra and Elston Howard tried to restrain Martin as Jackson yelled, "You never wanted me on this team anyway."

Watching the meltdown on television in Florida, Yankees Owner George Steinbrenner prepared to fire Martin. After a hastily called meeting, Martin and Jackson made an uncomfortable truce, and afterward a chastised Martin finally batted Jackson fourth. Jackson and Martin proceeded to lead the Yankees to 100 wins. "I was just waiting for the right time to move Jackson," claimed Martin, reluctant to praise the slugger.

Jackson responded by crushing the ball down the stretch, capping his redemption with his famous three-home run game in the World Series against the Los Angeles Dodgers and earning the nickname "Mr. October."

MAN TO MAN

Finley

Kuhn

FIGHTING THE POWER

Charles Finley was an owner, innovator and agitator, but not necessarily in that order. As owner of the Athletics franchise, he liked to win, even if it meant making those around him miserable in the process. At first, he focused his bile on players, angering them with contentious contract talks and cost-cutting measures. Players complained that the World Series rings he awarded during the Athletics' dynastic run in the 1970s looked like they were plucked out of a bubblegum machine.

His most public feud was an ongoing battle with MLB Commissioner Bowie Kuhn. The *tete-a-tete* began in earnest during the 1973 World Series, won by Finley's club. After second baseman Mike Andrews made a pair of 12th-inning errors in a Game 2 loss, Finley concocted a shoulder injury so he could replace the infielder with Manny Trillo for the remainder of the Series.

Kuhn fined Finley $7,000 for assorted World Series infractions, $5,000 of which was owed as reparations for the Andrews caper. Finley promptly counter-sued to have the fine repealed. When Oakland's reign at the top ended, it only increased the problems between the two.

After the A's lost hurler Catfish Hunter to free agency because Finley didn't pay the premiums on an insurance annuity, the owner became pro-active. In June 1976, he sold Vida Blue to the Yankees and shipped Joe Rudi and Rollie Fingers to the Red Sox. Citing the "best interests of baseball" clause, Kuhn voided the deals. Finley challenged Kuhn, saying he "didn't have the guts to stop him." By that time, his Oakland teams were struggling mightily, and Finley halted himself by selling the team before the 1981 season.

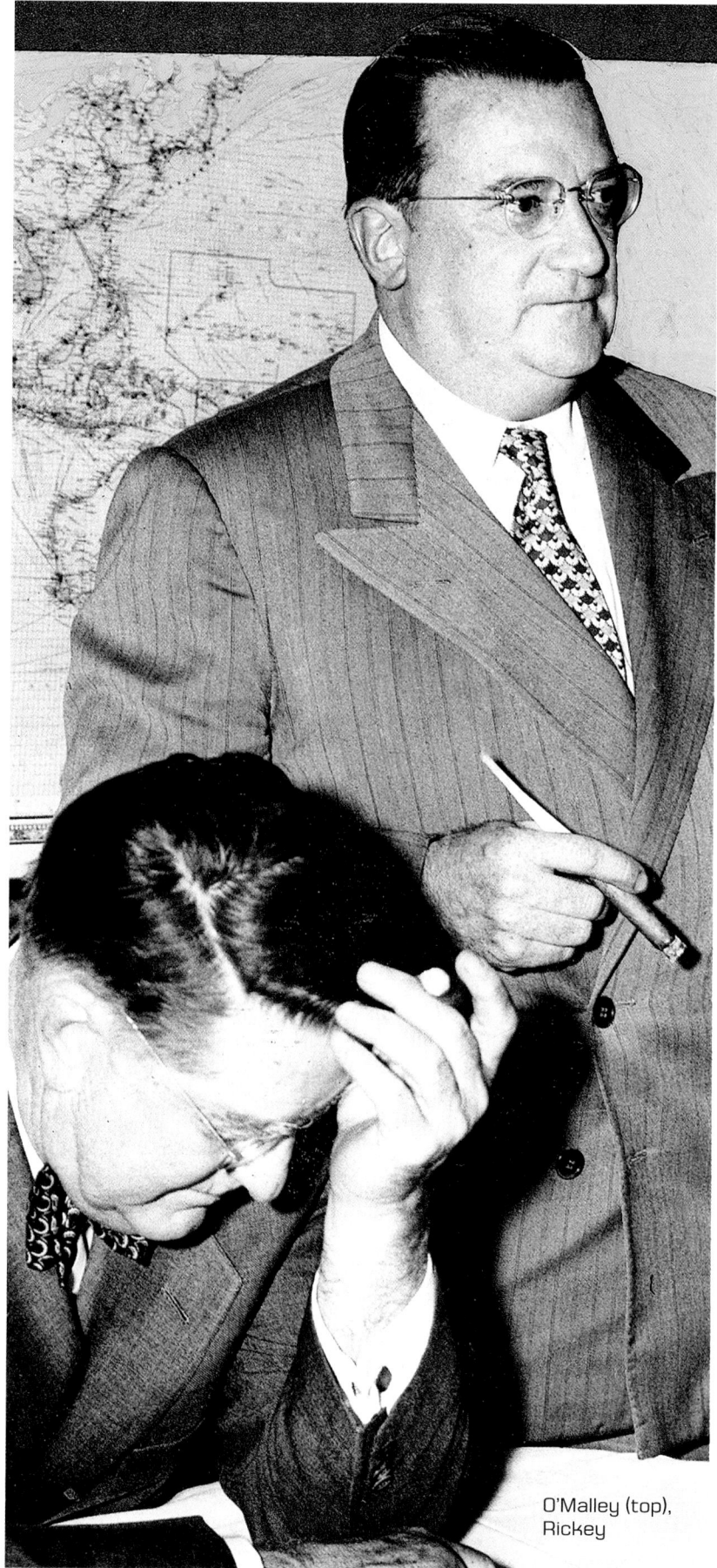

O'Malley (top), Rickey

DOMESTIC DISPUTE

Both shrewd businessmen, Branch Rickey and Walter O'Malley could each fill a room with his ego, which meant that no matter how fruitful their partnership, it was always going to have an expiration date.

O'Malley lured Rickey away from St. Louis in 1942. Rickey was the father of the modern farm system, and during his tenure with the Dodgers, the farm system was integral to the team's successes in the 1940s and '50s. The club won pennants in 1947 and 1949, losing in the World Series to the Yankees on each occasion. A key component of those pennant-winning teams was Jackie Robinson. That O'Malley and Rickey were willing to break the color barrier by signing Jackie Robinson defined their legacy.

The move transcended social barriers, but it also made the Dodgers better on the field. Rickey wanted to win. O'Malley was a bottom-line man. For a time, both goals dovetailed.

"He never went into a locker room in his life," *Los Angeles Times* columnist Jim Murray wrote of O'Malley. "He had come to the Dodgers as a caretaker for the company that held the mortgage on the club."

Despite winning consistently and drawing more than 1 million fans annually to Ebbets Field, the Dodgers were pinched financially because of Rickey's expanding farm system. Rickey and O'Malley also hadn't seen eye to eye over the drama surrounding Leo Durocher in the late 1940s. In 1950, Rickey telephoned O'Malley, informing him that he was selling his Dodgers stock for $1.025 million.

After their separation, each continued to show his talents. Rickey laid the foundation for the 1960 world champion Pirates and O'Malley, a visionary who tried to get a domed stadium in Brooklyn before he gave up haggling with city officials, changed baseball forever by moving his Dodgers to the West Coast and convincing the rival Giants to join him.

MAN TO MAN

PINT-SIZED POWER STRUGGLE

Two of baseball's smallest players created one of the biggest debates of their era. Who would you rather have: the New York Yankees' 5-foot-6, 150-pound Phil Rizzuto or the Brooklyn Dodgers' 5-foot-10, 160-pound Pee Wee Reese?

In 1941, the debate raged in New York, with neither team's fans willing to budge even an inch, and it continued for the better part of a decade. The reality is that there was no wrong answer, only a matter of taste. Most scouts believed that Rizzuto had a slightly better glove, but Reese could hit. He was a key part of a Brooklyn Dodgers' lineup that included Duke Snider. Rizzuto was a joker in the clubhouse — a foreshadowing of his terrific broadcasting career with the Yankees — but let his scrappy style speak for itself on the field. Reese was more of a traditional leader, and his willingness to accept and embrace Jackie Robinson as a teammate helped accelerate the sport's desegregation.

Rizzuto earned the nickname "Scooter" because the blur of his short legs as he ran made it look like he was scooting around the bases. But he was more Dustin Pedroia than Fred Patek. In 1950, he won the American League MVP Award, hitting .324 with a .418 on-base percentage and seven home runs. The scant power speaks to how well-rounded the rest of his game was. Reese was nothing if not consistent, earning 10 All-Star berths. He was thin, a little lanky. Rizzuto was stocky with wavy black hair.

The pair became friends through competition. When Reese was elected to the Hall of Fame in 1984, Rizzuto was initially disappointed. "I thought we would go in together," he said. Rizzuto, praised as a small man with a big heart by columnists, eventually earned election in 1994.

"If Rizzuto was the Red Sox's shortstop, we'd have won all those pennants, not the Yankees," said Ted Williams.

TALE OF THE TAPE: REESE'S AND RIZZUTO'S CAREER STATS										
Player	G	R	H	2B	3B	HR	RBI	SB	BB	AVG
Reese	2,166	1,338	2,170	330	80	126	885	232	1,210	.269
Rizzuto	1,661	877	1,588	239	62	38	563	149	651	.273

Reese (left), Rizzuto

MAN TO MAN

Ryan

Carlton

AGELESS ACES

Thirty became the new 20 in the early 1980s, as ageless aces Nolan Ryan and Steve Carlton continued to excel. Not surprisingly, they were among the first hurlers to incorporate physical fitness routines between starts. At a time when retirement should have been looming, Ryan and Carlton spent the summer of 1983 leapfrogging each other as the game's all-time strikeout leader. Walter Johnson had held the K's record for 62 years, but after Ryan first passed Johnson on April 22, 1983, it seemed to change hands weekly.

Known as "The Express," Ryan was 36 at the time and the media-averse Carlton — who answered to "Lefty" — was 38 and telling anyone who would listen that he would play 10 more years. When Ryan first broke Johnson's mark, he was still known for power, his fastball regularly flirting with the 100-mph mark.

"He was one of only two guys that I moved in the batter's box for and it wasn't forward," former American League MVP Don Baylor said.

Carlton insisted that he wasn't trying to strike hitters out, but hitters would be surprised at that admission. Even at 38, he led the league in strikeouts, his 275 easily besting Ryan's 183.

"Hitting his slider," said Pirates great Willie Stargell, "was like trying to eat soup with a fork."

Carlton's hold on history quickly slipped through his fingers. By 1985, he was barely hanging on in the Majors. Ryan found new life, ending the decade with a 301-strikeout season in 1989. It was part of one of baseball's best finishing kicks as he ended his career with 5,714 strikeouts.

TALE OF THE TAPE: RYAN'S AND CARLTON'S CAREER STATS									
Player	W-L	ERA	CG	SHO	SV	IP	BB	SO	WHIP
Ryan	324-292	3.19	222	61	3	5,386	2,795	5,714	1.247
Carlton	329-244	3.22	254	55	2	5,217.2	1,833	4,136	1.247

chapter 5
YANKEES-DODGERS

The rivalry between the Yankees and the Dodgers remains vibrant because these clubs have rarely met outside the World Series. Whether settling arguments over which borough, coast or league reigned supreme, the stakes have almost always been high when these teams have tangled. Aside from frequently taking place on the sport's greatest stage, this rivalry has also included some of the game's best players and most colorful personalities. It has featured the Duke vs. the Mick; given us Billy Martin and Tommy Lasorda; and has even produced "Dem Bums" and Mr. October.

ARMY OF ONE

It was a testament to the Yankees' run of World Series dominance that they were favored in the 1963 Fall Classic, despite staring down the barrel at Sandy Koufax's darting fastball and wicked curveball. The Dodgers' ace twirled 11 shutouts during an unforgettable '63 campaign and set a modern National League record with 306 strikeouts. But everyone thought that the Yankees had their own version of Koufax in Whitey Ford.

With Koufax winning both his starts in complete-game fashion, Los Angeles swept the Yankees. In leading the Dodgers to their second World Series title since moving to California, he struck out 23 batters and issued just three walks. His performance in the '63 Series hardly seemed possible when he struggled to find the strike zone while pitching for the Nathan's Famous amateur team as a teenager in Brooklyn. But Koufax overcame his youthful wildness, and from 1961–66 earned the nickname the "Left Arm of God."

"Either he throws the fastest ball I've ever seen," said frequent opponent Richie Ashburn, "or I'm going blind."

Before 69,000 fans at Yankee Stadium in Game 1, the 27-year-old struck out a then-record 15 batters in a complete-game victory. Said former record-holder Carl Erskine, "When I struck out 14 Yankees in 1953, I hit a peak of determination I never reached before or afterward. But Koufax striking out 15 is a normal performance for him."

In the Series-clincher, Koufax struck out eight with no walks in nine innings of work to lead the Dodgers to a 2-1 victory. Not surprisingly, he was named World Series MVP. Shortly thereafter, he received a sports car during an award presentation in New York. That's when the Big Apple exacted its revenge, with a policeman actually ticketing the new car for being on the sidewalk as it was presented to Koufax.

Koufax

YANKEES–DODGERS

Barber (with microphone)

BROOKLYN'S BARBER

For many fans in Brooklyn, broadcaster Red Barber represented the Dodgers. The players changed from 1939–53 and success varied, but the voice of summer did not, as Barber painted a picture with words. His famous calls included, "Oh-HO DOC-tor!" for great plays, "sitting in the catbird seat" when the team owned a big lead and "tied up in a crocus sack" for a sewn-up game. While he had a penchant for colloquialisms, Barber's professionalism defined him, and he never resorted to pandering partisanship.

As *The New York Times* wrote upon his passing, "He knew the difference between color and shtick." Barber never referred to the Dodgers as "us" or "we" — a prelude to his surprising switch from "Dem Bums" to the Yankees.

By 1953, Barber could no longer abide by the overbearing rules of Dodgers Owner Walter O'Malley, so he resigned. To the chagrin of the Flatbush faithful, Barber joined the Yankees and worked alongside legendary broadcaster Mel Allen. Both men were eventually elected to the Hall of Fame in 1978.

"I wasn't a Dodger fan. I wasn't a Yankee fan," Barber said. "I wasn't a fan of anyone. I described the game the best way I knew how without partiality. I think the listeners appreciated that."

As a Yankees broadcaster, Barber was every bit as good as he had been in Brooklyn. He was behind the microphone for baseball's first night game and the first televised game, too. Still, he's remembered more for his time in Brooklyn, where his voice was the soundtrack to people's lives.

"He is," said Vin Scully, who followed Barber as the iconic voice of the Dodgers, "perhaps the most literate sports announcer I have ever met."

Ebbets Field

BILLY'S GRAB

Before Billy Martin was a temperamental manager — who fought bar patrons, a marshmallow salesman and Reggie Jackson — Yankees Manager Casey Stengel described him as "the best little player I ever had. He did everything I asked."

Stengel and his wife never had children. But he treated his favorite players like sons, namely Mickey Mantle, Yogi Berra and Martin. A pedestrian .257 hitter during his career in the regular season, Martin had a knack for coming through in the biggest moments during the World Series.

In 1952, the Yankees met the Dodgers in the Fall Classic, and the teams split the first six games. In Game 7 in Brooklyn, Stengel turned to left-handed pitcher Bob Kuzava to face Duke Snider with the bases loaded. With one out in the seventh, Snider popped up, bringing Jackie Robinson to the plate. On the first pitch, Kuzava fooled him with a curve, inducing a pop fly high into the westerly wind blowing in from left field. Martin gave chase, relentlessly pursing the fly ball as it dropped. Just as Dodgers baserunners Carl Furillo and Billy Cox were racing toward the plate, Martin made a game-saving catch at his shoetops, pushing the Yankees to the brink of their fourth straight World Series title.

A year later, Martin belted 12 World Series hits as the Yankees won their fifth straight title (three of them at Brooklyn's expense), but his catch in '52 sticks in the minds of Dodgers fans.

"We won by just that," said Stengel, holding his thumb and forefinger a half-inch apart to symbolize the difference in the Series — Martin's grab.

YANKEES–DODGERS

Jackson

JACKSON'S CAREER POSTSEASON STATS					
G	AB	HR	RBI	AVG	OPS
77	281	18	48	.278	.885

MR. OCTOBER

Shortly after Yankees Owner George Steinbrenner acquired Reggie Jackson as a free agent in November 1976, the slugger made headlines for his mouth. But it was the volume of his bat that had brought him to New York. Having earned AL MVP honors with the Oakland Athletics and helped the team to titles in 1972, '73 and '74, Jackson had long proven that he could walk the walk as well as he could talk the talk. Forced to establish an uneasy truce with skipper Billy Martin after nearly coming to blows in the dugout during the 1977 season, Jackson took off when he was finally moved to the cleanup spot over the final two months. He hit 10 homers with a .304 average from Sept. 1 through the end of the season, and appeared primed to dominate in October as he had with the A's. Although the Yankees emerged triumphant from the ALCS, Jackson struggled to make his mark and was forced to watch teammates deliver the most stirring moments.

Through the first three games of the Fall Classic, the Dodgers' pitching staff kept Jackson in check. But he began to break out with a homer in both Games 4 and 5. With the Yankees ahead of the Dodgers, 3-games-to-2, and a capacity crowd at Yankee Stadium eager to celebrate the team's first title since 1962, Jackson hit nearly 40 home runs in batting practice. After Jackson's BP fireworks, he walked in his first at-bat. With the Yankees trailing, 3-2, in the fourth, Jackson homered off Burt Hooton, depositing a fastball into the seats. In the fifth, Jackson stepped in against Elias Sosa, who tried to sneak a low, outside fastball past the slugger. He yanked the pitch over the right-field fence.

Two down, history to go. With another home run, Jackson would tie Babe Ruth's single-game World Series record. Charlie Hough's knuckleball in the eighth didn't stand a chance as Jackson swatted it 450 feet. Three swings, three home runs, and a nickname earned: Mr. October. If you count his eighth-inning blast in Game 5, Jackson had homered on his last four swings. Dodgers first baseman Steve Garvey later admitted that he was clapping in his glove as Jackson rounded the bases in the eighth.

"Three home runs," Jackson told Martin in the celebratory clubhouse. "Do you realize I just did that?"

YANKEES–DODGERS

Amoros

BUMS NO MORE

The Brooklyn Dodgers finished no lower than second in the NL in any year from 1949–55. But there was a gnawing pang in the gut of every player and fan over what they hadn't won during those impressive years: a championship.

Beginning in 1916, the Dodgers appeared in seven World Series and lost them all, including five times to the rival Yankees. In 1955, it looked like more of the same when they fell behind to the Bombers, 2 games to none. A 21-run outburst over the next three games put the Dodgers on the brink of a title, but Yankees ace Whitey Ford dominated Game 6, forcing a winner-take-all seventh game.

In the bottom of the sixth with the Dodgers leading, 2-0, fun-loving, fleet-footed Sandy Amoros entered as a defensive replacement in left field. With runners on first and second and no outs, Yankees catcher Yogi Berra strode to the plate. He knifed a line-drive down the left-field line. Shading Berra in the gap, Amoros didn't appear to have a chance. The 5-foot-7 speedster — in 1952, Amoros was considered the game's fastest player — raced across the grass and snared the ball in his outstretched right hand. Recognizing the situation — that the runners were on the move — Amoros whipped the ball to shortstop Pee Wee Reese who fired to first baseman Gil Hodges for a double play. The Yankees never threatened again, and Amoros's effort was coined "the million dollar catch" seeing as it led to the Bums' lone title and the winners' purse that went with it.

Brooklyn's famed "Boys of Summer" included some of the most memorable players in baseball's golden age, but the little-known Amoros delivered the club's greatest triumph. The Cuban left fielder's catch in Game 7 clinched the franchise's only championship in Brooklyn. Asked about it years later, Amoros, who died at age 62 in 1992, said succinctly, "It's really too good to describe."

YANKEES-DODGERS

PERFECTION

A look at the back of Don Larsen's baseball card does not reveal an ace. Two seasons removed from posting an unsightly 3-21 record for the Baltimore Orioles, Larsen prepared for the 1956 season with the Yankees by making headlines for a Spring Training car accident. An 11-5 regular season was encouraging but hardly seemed a harbinger of greatness. After he was shelled by the Dodgers in Game 2 of the '56 World Series, Larsen looked an unlikely candidate to produce a heroic Series performance. In fact, when Larsen entered the Yankees' clubhouse prior to Game 5, he didn't expect to pitch again in a big spot.

During the '56 season, a Yankees pitcher never knew for sure if he was going to start a given game until he found a baseball in one of his cleats when he turned up at the clubhouse just hours before the first pitch. Considering his meek effort earlier in the Series, Larsen figured he would be skipped when he arrived at the stadium on the day of Game 5. But there was a ball waiting in his shoe. Larsen took a nap in the trainer's room to prep for his unexpected assignment.

Refreshed, the pitcher was sharp early, but hardly dominant as the Dodgers kept getting good wood on the ball. Larsen required solid glovework from his teammates to keep his bid for history alive. Shortstop Gil McDougald robbed Jackie Robinson of a hit, making a lunging grab of a deflected line drive in the second inning. With the Yankees leading, 2-0, after seven frames, Larsen was aware of the history he was writing and calmed his nerves with a cigarette. During the game, he asked teammate Mickey Mantle if he thought he could pull it off. Mantle, adhering to baseball tradition, didn't say a word.

After Larsen breezed through the eighth, three outs stood between the right-hander and immortality. Carl Furillo flied out to right field and Roy Campanella grounded out to second base. That brought up Dale Mitchell, a contact hitter who had struck out just 119 times in his long, distinguished career. Larsen ran the count to 1-2 before striking Mitchell out with a fastball. Larsen finished with 97 pitches, 71 strikes and the only perfect game in the history of the World Series.

Yogi Berra (8), Larsen

YANKEES–DODGERS WORLD SERIES MATCHUPS, 1941–56

Year	Winner
1941	Yankees (4-1)
1947	Yankees (4-3)
1949	Yankees (4-1)
1952	Yankees (4-3)
1953	Yankees (4-2)
1955	Dodgers (4-3)
1956	Yankees (4-3)

YANKEES–DODGERS

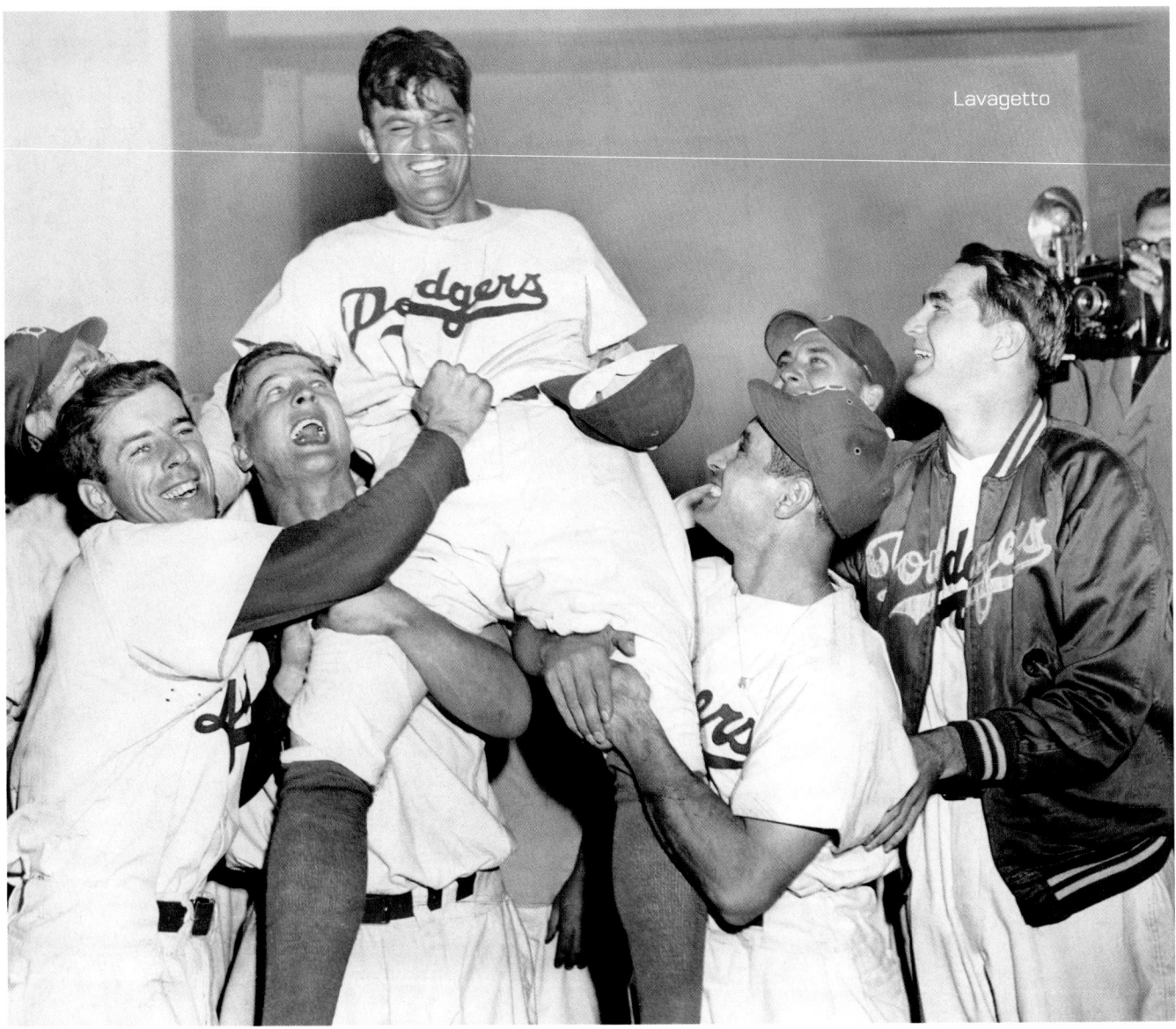

Lavagetto

NOT QUITE A NO-NO

Before Don Larsen's perfect game for the Yankees in the 1956 World Series, there was Bill Bevens' painful near-miss, when he lost a ballgame, a no-hitter and, technically, his career on a single pitch. Effectively wild at times, Bevens was an erratic starting pitcher who had accomplished little during the 1947 season. Tapped to start Game 4 of the '47 World Series, he was just supposed to keep the Yankees close. But he did even better than that. Through eight innings, Bevens hadn't allowed a single hit to the Dodgers in what was clearly the performance of his life. True to his tightrope style, though, Bevens had already issued eight walks to heighten the suspense.

With one out in the ninth, the chess match began. Bevens walked Carl Furillo, but then got Spider Jorgensen to pop up. That brought pinch-hitter Pete Reiser to the plate and Al Gionfriddo in as a pinch-runner. Gionfriddo shocked everyone by stealing second, just his third stolen base on the year. Bevens then intentionally walked Reiser. Dodgers Manager Burt Shotton countered by pinch-hitting Cookie Lavagetto for Eddie Stanky. Lavagetto had 18 hits all season in a limited role, and Bevens needed just one more out to secure the win and his place in the record books. He couldn't sneak a fastball past Lavagetto, though, who lined a shot off the right-field wall. The runners were moving on the pitch, scoring easily to give the Dodgers the win.

In an odd twist to a remarkable contest, neither Lavagetto nor Bevens ever appeared in the Major Leagues again after the 1947 World Series.

Owen (catching)

ONE THAT GOT AWAY

Entering the 1941 season, the Brooklyn Dodgers had not played in a World Series in more than two decades. Before they captured the NL pennant that year, they were developing a reputation based more on eccentric personalities than victories. But pitted against the Yankees for the first time on the game's grand stage, the Dodgers had a shot until a wayward pitch late in Game 4.

The Dodgers led, 4-3, at Ebbets Field, needing just one out to knot the Series at two games apiece. Reliever Hugh Casey was facing Tommy Henrich with no one on base and the Yankees seemingly having little chance.

With two strikes, Casey nodded when All-Star catcher Mickey Owen signaled for a breaking pitch. Owen figured Casey would throw his sharp breaking slider. Instead, he delivered an overhand curve that caught Henrich — and Owen — off guard. Henrich swung and missed badly. Owen stabbed at the ball, but it hit off of his glove and rolled away from him. Henrich raced to first base safely. Instead of the game being over, the Yankees' rally was just beginning.

"It really broke big, in and down. Tommy missed it by six inches," Owen said.

Added Henrich, "It fooled me so much I figured maybe it fooled Mickey, too."

Joe DiMaggio followed with a single, paving the way for Charlie Keller's go-ahead double. After Joe Gordon's extra-base hit, the Yankees breezed to a 7-4 victory. The Yankees would go on to clinch the Series in five games. Owen, fortunately, was not vilified for his untimely mistake.

"I had offers of jobs and proposals of marriage. Some girls sent their pictures in bathing suits, and my wife tore them up," Owen told *The Saturday Evening Post*.

YANKEES–DODGERS

Garvey, Yeager, Steve Howe and Derrel Thomas (left to right)

GOING DOWN

In a contentious year defined by labor strife that shortened the Major League season to approximately 110 games, it was fitting that two clubs with no love lost between them faced off in the hotly contested 1981 World Series. Even after a shortened season, the Dodgers and Yankees had plenty of ammunition to draw on when getting fired up to face one another. There was equal distaste on both sides, if not an equal number of victories. In the previous 10 World Series matchups between the two clubs, going back to when it had been an all-New York affair, the Dodgers had won just twice. Los Angeles was still stinging from its back-to-back failures in 1977 and 1978, and when the club dropped the first two games of the '81 Series to New York, it looked like another familiar ending was approaching. But Fernando Valenzuela, the Dodgers' sensational rookie pitcher from Mexico, changed the script.

With the Yankees' Reggie Jackson sidelined by a calf injury, Valenzuela delivered a complete-game, 5-4 victory in Game 3. Jackson returned for Game 4, posting three hits, but also lost a critical fly ball in the sun in an 8-7 Dodgers' win. The outcome of Game 4 led Yankees Owner George Steinbrenner to issue a 10 p.m. curfew to keep his players from tiring themselves out with a night on the town. Turns out it wasn't his players he had to worry about. Riding an elevator at the Hyatt Wilshire Hotel down to dinner, Steinbrenner said he was confronted by unruly Dodgers fans on the seventh floor. Steinbrenner alleged they told him to "go back to those animals in New York and take those choking ballplayers with you!" A physical fight ensued, and though struck by a beer bottle, Steinbrenner claimed to have won with a left-right combo that broke his right hand.

Led by a group of young players that skipper Tommy Lasorda helped raise in the farm system, the Dodgers weren't distracted by the unfortunate off-field action. Homegrown L.A. stalwarts Steve Garvey, Davey Lopes, Bill Russell and Ron Cey guided the Dodgers to an easy 9-2 victory in the deciding sixth game. Cey, Steve Yeager and Pedro Guerrero shared MVP honors, marking the first time teammates received the honor together.

chapter 6
PLAYOFF RIVALS

Although the World Series deservedly garners much of the postseason attention, the Division Series and League Championship Series are just as important to making October the most memorable month on the sporting calendar. While qualifying for the postseason itself is quite an accomplishment, teams take the field for the earlier rounds of the playoffs intent on reaching the Fall Classic. With a pennant hanging in the balance, emotions are bound to run hot, especially when certain clubs find themselves paired repeatedly over the years — like the Cincinnati Reds and Pittsburgh Pirates in the 1970s and the Kansas City Royals and New York Yankees in the late 1970s and early 1980s. Rival teams may get on each other's nerves during the regular season, but they are out for blood come October.

GRAND SLAM SINGLE

Embroiled in a heated north-south rivalry long before the calendar flipped to October 1999, the Mets and Braves staged a grudge match in that year's NLCS. The classic postseason confrontation was defined by extra innings, bile and unexpected twists. It was the series that forever identified Mets third baseman Robin Ventura, who was known for his 18 career grand slams, with his "grand slam single."

The Mets had lost Games 1 through 3 by a combined four runs but managed a 3-2 win in Game 4 to stay alive. After 5 hours and 46 minutes had passed in a rainy Game 5, Ventura stepped in against Atlanta reliever Kevin McGlinchy with the bases loaded in the bottom of the 15th and the score tied, 3-3. The Mets were facing elimination, and Ventura was just 1 for 18 in the series when he rifled a shot over the right-center field wall at Shea Stadium. The capacity crowd went berserk. Backup catcher Todd Pratt, who had been on first when Ventura came up, was as caught up in the moment as the delirious fans. After touching second base, he raced back and embraced Ventura. By leaving the basepaths and stopping Ventura, Pratt's embrace turned the walk-off grand slam into a game-winning single.

Game 6 proved to be nearly as dramatic, as a home run by Mike Piazza helped the Mets erase a five-run deficit. But they squandered a 9-8 lead in the 10th and then watched their dreams disappear in the 11th. After intentional walks to Chipper Jones and Brian Jordan, Mets pitcher Kenny Rogers was left to face young Andruw Jones when something nearly as strange as a grand slam single happened. Jones, the teenager who had debuted just weeks earlier, worked the count full. Then he kept the bat on his shoulder and drew a walk-off walk.

"Andruw usually swings at that pitch five feet outside," Braves hitting instructor Don Baylor said.

The suddenly patient Braves outfielder summed it up: "Those last two games are probably the best two games you are going to see in a long time."

Ventura

PLAYOFF RIVALS

HOME OF THE BRAVE

With Barry Bonds, Andy Van Slyke and Bobby Bonilla in the outfield, Jim Leyland's Pittsburgh Pirates were the cream of the NL East crop in the early 1990s. In 1991 and '92, the Bucs challenged the Atlanta Braves for the right to represent the National League in the World Series. Each hard-fought NLCS matchup ended up going the distance, with seven of the 14 games in those two years decided by just one or two runs.

In 1991, Van Slyke homered in Game 1 as the Pirates rolled to a 5-1 win. But Steve Avery twirled a gem for the Braves in Game 2, and his team then won Game 3. After close wins in Games 4 and 5, the Pirates looked poised to deliver a knockout blow. But the Braves' pitchers held the Pirates scoreless through the final 22 innings of the series, overcoming a 3-games-to-2 deficit.

After coming up just short in the 1991 World Series, the Braves arrived in the '92 NLCS with unfinished business. Waiting for them once more were the Pirates. After teetering on the brink of elimination, Pittsburgh won Games 5 and 6 to force a Game 7. Staked to a 2-0 lead in the ninth inning of the decisive contest, Pittsburgh could not close it out. Francisco Cabrera drove home the tying and winning runs for Atlanta, and Braves first baseman Sid Bream scored the series-clinching run in iconic fashion by beating out a throw from Bonds in a dramatic play at the plate.

OUTFIELD ASSIST

A 12-year-old usually has a better chance of becoming a baseball hero in Williamsport, Pa., than Yankee Stadium, but October can create some unlikely stars. In the eighth inning of the first game of the 1996 American League Championship Series, Jeffrey Maier was just watching his favorite team when, in an instant, his life changed forever. Yankees rookie shortstop Derek Jeter lofted a fly ball to deep right, and Orioles right fielder Tony Tarasco raced back to the wall, raising his glove. Maier reached out with his mitt, deflecting the ball into the stands. Replays showed that the ball could have been caught by Tarasco for the second out of the eighth inning. Instead, umpire Rich Garcia ruled it a game-tying home run, a pivotal moment in the Yankees' march toward winning the AL pennant and eventually the 1996 World Series.

A random fan put Maier on his shoulders as the crowd cheered him. He was dubbed "Angel in the Outfield" in local headlines and appeared on *Live With Regis and Kathie Lee* and ABC's *Good Morning America*. Many parents and coaches were uneasy with the celebration of a kid who broke the rules to help the home team.

"I didn't mean to do anything bad," Maier said. "I'm just a 12-year-old kid trying to catch a ball."

Baltimore players, obviously, weren't so forgiving.

"If one of the Orioles had hit it, he would have been strung up on Throggs Neck Bridge," said Orioles outfielder Bobby Bonilla, who knew New York well, having played with the Mets.

Years later, Maier became a successful player at Wesleyan College. Although he was often heckled by fans of opposing teams, Maier seemed to have a sense of humor about his place in baseball lore. He even participated in a student film about himself and an Orioles fan titled *I Hate Jeffrey Maier*.

"I have no regrets about it," Maier said.

Maier (in stands)

PLAYOFF RIVALS

Ramirez

FAMILIAR FOES

Playoff mainstays throughout the 2000s, the Los Angeles Angels and Boston Red Sox collided in four AL Division Series during a decade in which both clubs celebrated World Series triumphs. While the Angels claimed the crown in 2002 without having to cross the Sox, Boston had to pass through Anaheim en route to its titles in 2004 and '07.

Powered by the formidable one-two punch of David Ortiz and Manny Ramirez in the heart of the batting order, the Sox swept the Angels in those two meetings. In those series, the All-Star pair combined to hit six home runs — Big Papi even clinched the '04 ALDS with a walk-off homer — and drive in 18 runs in six games.

The 2008 ALDS was another story, with three games being decided by two runs or fewer. True to form, though, the Sox ultimately prevailed on a walk-off single by Jed Lowrie in Game 4. When the teams met for a third straight season in 2009, the Angels were determined to finally flip the script. They did just that by sweeping the Red Sox in breathtaking fashion, storming back in the ninth inning of Game 3 at Fenway Park to stun Red Sox Nation. Collectively, the Sox hit a paltry .158 for the series, getting swept for just the third time since Division Series play was instituted in 1995 and missing the chance to appear in a third consecutive American League Championship Series.

Fueled by energized crowds on both coasts and on-field contempt bred by playoff familiarity, these series certainly never wanted for intensity, even when the drama was lacking. In their four combined ALDS matchups over just six postseasons, the Red Sox won nine of 13 games.

PLAYOFF RIVALS

Blue

PITCHERS' DUELS

From 1970–75, the Baltimore Orioles and Oakland A's combined to hog nine of the 12 available spots in the American League Championship Series, competing against one another three times during that span. It became a familiar sight to see either green and gold or orange and white on the field when a trip to the World Series was on the line.

Behind their historic quartet of 20-game winners — Mike Cuellar, Pat Dobson, Jim Palmer and Dave McNally — the O's swept the first matchup in 1971. While the Orioles watched the playoffs from their nests the following year, the A's won the '72 AL pennant and then outlasted the Reds in the Fall Classic.

When they squared off again in 1973, Oakland, the reigning champion, featured Reggie Jackson and a formidable group of starters in Ken Holtzman, Vida Blue and Catfish Hunter. The '73 series went the distance — five games — as the Athletics prevailed and exacted their revenge on Baltimore for 1971. The two teams hit a combined .205 in the series in the face of some expectedly dominant pitching. After besting Baltimore, the Athletics would sneak by the Mets in seven games to claim their second world championship.

The following season, both clubs returned to the ALCS stage and, just like in earlier matchups, pitching was the lead story. The two teams managed to score just 18 total runs in the four-game series, hitting a combined .180. As in the previous meeting, the Athletics came out victorious. Oakland emerged as a mid-decade dynasty by winning the World Series in both 1973 and '74, the second and third titles in a string of three consecutive championships.

PLAYOFF RIVALS

KING GEORGE

From their expansion roots, the Kansas City Royals blossomed into the Yankees' bitter rivals during the mid-1970s. Founded in 1969, the Royals quickly became contenders, playing in four American League Championship Series from 1976–80. While the Yankees barely edged the Royals in aggregate wins in those matchups, 9-8, they held a commanding 3-1 lead in series wins.

All rivalries need a stirring opening act, and it is hard to top Chris Chambliss's walk-off home run to clinch the '76 ALCS for the Yankees. It created a veritable riot at Yankee Stadium, with fans storming the field and leaving Chambliss unable to touch home plate. That blast ignited a run of three straight ALCS victories over the Royals. Although Chambliss and his teammates consistently came through when the stakes were highest, Hall of Famer George Brett shined so brightly for the Royals that he left the biggest mark on the rivalry. In Game 3 of the '78 ALCS, Brett slugged three home runs off Catfish Hunter, yet the Royals still lost the game when Thurman Munson delivered a 475-foot homer of his own in the eighth inning.

Brett torched the Yankees' pitchers, going 24 for 67 during all those ALCS matchups with six home runs and 14 RBI. It spoke to the many layers of this instant rivalry that Brett's most impactful play might have been a heads-up defensive gem in Game 2 in 1980. When the Royals' Willie Wilson overthrew the cutoff man after a base hit in the top of the eighth inning, Brett wisely backed it up, wheeling and nailing Willie Randolph easily at the plate to preserve a 3-2 lead. The Royals completed a sweep the next day. It was a necessary punctuation mark in this rivalry — a hint of equality.

Santana

NO ESCAPE FROM NEW YORK

It's tough to imagine one team bedeviling another in October as much as the Yankees haunted the Twins during the 2000s. Meeting four times in the American League Division Series from 2003–10, New York won 12 of the 14 total games played between these teams. In fact, just one Minnesota pitcher started a game that wasn't won by New York: Johan Santana started the Twins' wins in the opening games of both the 2003 and 2004 ALDS.

On days when the 2004 and '06 AL Cy Young winner wasn't on the hill, Minnesota had no kryptonite for the Yankees' super bats. The Bombers scored 68 runs in those 12 wins against the Twins — the equivalent of a 918-run pace over the course of a full season.

"This is not much fun at all, to come up here, being knocked out, knowing your season is over with again after three games in the playoffs," Minnesota Manager Ron Gardenhire said after the Twins were swept by the Bombers in 2010. "We've had that a few times."

Indeed, though the Twins made the playoffs six times from 2002–10, all of their postseason appearances ended without a trip to the World Series. What's more, five of the six appearances ended with a defeat in the ALDS. The Yankees, on the other hand, made two trips to the World Series during that time frame, winning it all in 2009 after once again bypassing the Twins.

PLAYOFF RIVALS

Lofton

RED DAWN

Following the labor strike in 1994 that left baseball without a World Series for the first time in 90 years, MLB returned having added a quirk to a playoff format that had been unchanged for nearly a quarter-century before. Doubling in size, the postseason now featured eight teams — four from each league — competing for a chance to claim the Commissioner's Trophy. In the years following that transition, the Boston Red Sox and Cleveland Indians became fixtures in the new American League Division Series, facing one another three times in the latter part of the 1990s.

In 1995, the Indians' powerful offense, featuring veteran mashers Albert Belle and Eddie Murray and an emerging tandem of stars in Manny Ramirez and Jim Thome, slugged its way past Boston in a three-game sweep. It wasn't until three years had passed — including two heart-wrenching World Series losses in '95 and '97 — that the Indians would get a shot at defeating Boston in the playoffs again. In 1998, the Red Sox took command early with an 11-3 pounding in Game 1, but the Indians were still armed with an explosive offense and, behind Ramirez and speedster Kenny Lofton, won the next three games to oust Boston once more.

The next season, however, the balance of power shifted. The Indians jumped out to a 2-games-to-none series lead, and it seemed like Boston was about to be swept in the LDS again. But then Boston's bats came alive, as the Red Sox scored 44 runs in the LDS's final three games — including 23 in a Game 4 romp. The highlight came when Pedro Martinez, that season's eventual AL Cy Young winner and normally a starting pitcher, completely overpowered Cleveland's 1,000-run offense in a six-inning relief appearance in Game 5, striking out eight and not allowing a single base hit. Ultimately, the Sox advanced to their first ALCS since 1990, though they would eventually succumb to the Yankees.

PLAYOFF RIVALS

INSEPARABLE

Just as the Athletics and Orioles hoarded the ALCS invites for most of the '70s, the Pirates and Reds were frequent October sparring partners in the NLCS during the same decade. Competing for the NL pennant six times each during the '70s, Pittsburgh and Cincinnati fielded some of the most unforgettable teams in their franchises' histories during this era. Unfortunately, such dominance often made the NLCS rather anticlimactic. Four of their combined NLCS appearances were three-game sweeps — including three against one another — while two others needed just four games.

The tendency for the hottest team to steamroll the opposition made the 1972 matchup all the more special. The Bucs were looking to defend their '71 World Series crown, but the Big Red Machine was just starting to fire on all cylinders. Led by Pete Rose, Joe Morgan and 24-year-old sensation Johnny Bench, the Reds' offense was relentless. The pitching wasn't bad, either, finishing the year third in the National League in ERA. It seemed fitting that the series went the full five games this time around.

Taking it one step further, this series was eventually decided in the ninth inning of Game 5, with enough drama to make up for what the other series lacked. Trailing, 3-2, with their season on the brink, the Reds sent Bench up to the plate to lead off against Pirates closer Dave Giusti. Bench had previously been just 3 for 18 off Giusti in his career before that fateful at-bat, when he tied the game with a solo home run. After chasing Giusti, the Reds went for the kill, putting runners on first and third base with two men down. With the winning run at third, new reliever Bob Moose uncorked a wild pitch, plating George Foster. The Reds would go on to lose the World Series that year, but would claim the '75 and '76 titles as their own. The Pirates won rings in '71 and '79, bookending a successful decade for two top clubs.

Rose (scoring)

chapter 7
WORLD SERIES RIVALS

After the American League broke onto the scene to challenge the National League in 1901, it took a few years before the rival circuits grudgingly settled into a peaceful coexistence. By that point, players and managers on each side of the divide burned for the chance to prove their league's superiority. Thanks to these competitive instincts — and the realization that fans would surely pay to witness such a spectacle — the World Series was born in 1903. Ever since, the Fall Classic has showcased the game's elite performers on its biggest stage. Certain teams have met time and again, developing a special animosity that blooms only in October, while others have arrived on the Fall Classic stage with pre-existing scores to settle.

THE I-70 SHOWDOWN

The Kansas City Royals weren't even supposed to be there. After all, they barely won their division crown in 1985 and were never expected to beat the Toronto Blue Jays for the pennant in the ALCS. But held together by chicken wire, duct tape and strong pitching, the Royals didn't flinch all season long.

Matched up against their intra-state foes in an I-70 World Series battle, the Royals were again in the underdog role. The Cardinals were baseball's bullies in 1985, posting 101 regular-season wins en route to the NL pennant. Behind terrific pitching performances by lefty John Tudor in Games 1 and 4, St. Louis jumped to a 3-games-to-1 Series lead. Celebrations were on tap at Busch Stadium and throughout the Gateway City, since just a handful of teams had ever rallied from such a deficit.

Taking a cue from stoic and intellectual skipper Dick Howser, the Royals remained calm despite facing elimination in Game 5, as Royals pitcher Danny Jackson and hot-hitting Willie Wilson made sure that the Royals survived to fight yet another day. Kansas City's 6-1 win set up Game 6, a contest that still leaves a bitter taste in the mouths of Cardinals' fans.

After both starters put up zeroes through seven innings, St. Louis scratched out a run in the eighth. Rookie reliever Todd Worrell looked to make the 1-0 lead stand up in the ninth inning. Then umpire Don Denkinger missed a call at first base. Royals outfielder Jorge Orta bounced a ball to first baseman Jack Clark and ran down the line. Clark fielded the ball and tossed it to Worrell, who was covering first. Worrell reached for the ball. It popped into his glove. And then Orta's lead foot stomped onto the bag. To everyone's shock, Denkinger signaled that he was safe.

"I had 30 great years and I had one call that's all anybody ever wants to talk about," Denkinger said years later.

With Orta safe at first, Kansas City rallied for a 2-1 win. After seeming to have the world championship sewn up, St. Louis was reeling, and the surging Royals flushed the Cardinals' title hopes away with an 11-0 drubbing in Game 7. Pitcher Bret Saberhagen earned MVP honors at age 21, thanks to two complete-game victories while allowing just a single run. The Series cast the teams in different lights — Kansas City as scrappy, St. Louis as petulant. In Game 7, St. Louis skipper Whitey Herzog admitted he wanted to get thrown out after Cardinals relief pitcher Joaquin Andujar complained to the umpire about the strike zone. Howser just sat back in the other dugout and watched as the Royals sent the Birds home for the winter.

WORLD SERIES RIVALS

1906 World Series

HITLESS IN CHICAGO

Chicago White Sox player-manager Fielder Jones will never be mistaken for longtime Orioles skipper Earl Weaver. Jones never saw the need — or, frankly, the players — to preach the virtues of the three-run home run during his stint at the helm of the Pale Hose in the first decade of the 20th century. The 1906 White Sox relied instead on opportunistic hitting and outstanding pitching to propel their title run after they managed just seven round-trippers all year. Using this formula, they won 19 straight games at one point to turn their season around.

Jones favored brains over brawn as he led the "Hitless Wonders" past the favored Chicago Cubs in the 1906 World Series. Frank Isbell and George Rohe combined for 15 hits to lead a Sox offense that didn't launch a single home run and had just 13 extra-base hits in the Series. As it had been all season long, the White Sox's starting pitchers were the story, leaving the Cubs' hottest hitters all wet. Ed Walsh won two games for the South Siders with a snapping spitball that would ultimately earn him induction into the Hall of Fame. Walsh was the kind of figure that deserved the spotlight, big and strong with matinee idol looks. He was once described as a man "who could strut while standing still," a quality that never endeared him to Chicago White Sox Owner Charles Comiskey.

Walsh went 2-0 in the Series, allowing just one earned run in 15 innings, providing an ideal complement to the work of Nick Altrock, who went 1-1 with two complete games while allowing just two earned runs. While the White Sox tamed the Cubs' famed Tinker-to-Evers-to-Chance infield trio, they were also resourceful at the plate under Jones' leadership.

"A White Sox rally," it was written, "is a base on balls, a sacrifice, a stolen base and a long fly."

BATTLE OF THE BAY

Proximity usually breeds some combination of respect, jealousy and animosity among professional sports teams. Having fans of each club mingling together throughout the shared region only stokes the flames. Before Interleague Play became an annual MLB ritual in 1997, the Oakland–San Francisco rivalry was only debated on bar stools and during Spring Training — when the teams faced off frequently.

The way Oakland firebrand Carney Lansford remembers the matchups, the Athletics didn't lose a single spring game. "We had our best lineup out there every time. I am not kidding. We wanted to beat them every time. Ownership made it clear that it was important. So when we reached the World Series, we knew we were going to beat them."

In 1989, the two teams appeared on a collision course for a hard-fought Fall Classic. Dominant LCS performances by each club led to endless hyping of the Series, billed as the "Battle of the Bay." Local fans and media compared San Francisco's Will Clark to Oakland's Rickey Henderson, dissected Clark's supposed dislike for teammate Jeffrey Leonard and accused Oakland closer Dennis Eckersley of scuffing the ball.

Yet the matchups and the personalities became irrelevant before Game 3 got underway at Candlestick Park. At 5:04 p.m. local time during warmups, an earthquake registering 7.1 on the Richter Scale rocked Northern California. The enormity of the event was terrifying, as news reports rolled in chronicling the destruction and loss of life in the area. A World Series that had infused the Bay with such passion and pride was an afterthought following the 15 seconds in which the ground shook. The Giants were already trailing, 2 games to none, when play was halted for 10 days. After the hiatus, the Athletics went on to sweep the Giants, but the victory celebration was relatively muted under the circumstances.

WORLD SERIES RIVALS

THE SUBWAY SERIES

By the start of the 2000 World Series, the New York Yankees were a steamroller, harkening back to the franchise's glory days in previous generations. The Bronx Bombers had won three of the previous four World Series — posting an alarming 12-2 record in those Fall Classics — when they went up against the crosstown Mets in pursuit of their 26th world title.

Championships had become as necessary as oxygen for Yankees Owner George Steinbrenner, but this one was even more critical, because a loss might cede the coveted back pages of the New York tabloids to the neighboring team. He pulled skipper Joe Torre aside, telling him, "We cannot afford to lose to the Mets. There's just too much at stake here for us."

But skipper Bobby Valentine's Mets felt like they had nothing to lose against the vaunted Yankees, and the upstarts infuriated the Yankees with their bravado. Mets outfielder Benny Agbayani predicted that his club, in the throes of a title drought since 1986, would win in five games. Once the outcome of the Series was determined — a five-game victory for the Bombers — Yankees reliever Jeff Nelson chortled in the champagne celebration at Shea Stadium, "Agbayani was right after all. He just got the wrong team."

Despite lasting just five games, the Series was incredibly hard-fought. The Yankees forced extras in Game 1 with a ninth-inning rally and won it in the 12th. The next game was another taut one-run affair, hanging in the balance in the final frame. Again, the result went the Yankees' way.

After the Bombers lost Game 3, Steinbrenner blamed the conditions of the visiting clubhouse at Shea Stadium. He had the couches and chairs from the Yankees' home clubhouse shipped across the city to make his team more comfortable. After going to all that trouble, the furniture was damaged in a flood in the Shea clubhouse during Game 4.

The Yankees ultimately won behind the core group of players that defined the club's 1990s dominance. Mariano Rivera saved the clincher with Bernie Williams and Derek Jeter hitting home runs. All told, the Yankees only outscored the Mets 19-16 in the Series. Nevertheless, several Yankees couldn't resist mocking their vanquished New York rivals by butchering a rendition of "Who Let the Dogs Out," the 2000 Mets' adopted theme song.

"I think our run of four World Series appearances in five years is pretty [darn] good," Torre said.

Torre (left), Valentine

WORLD SERIES RIVALS

Polo Grounds

HOME-FIELD ADVANTAGE

It's bad enough when neighboring franchises have to share the sports pages of the local papers. But it's even worse when the rivals have to share a home, as the Yankees and Giants did as co-tenants of the Polo Grounds from 1913–22. When the Yankees first moved to the Polo Grounds in Upper Manhattan, the Giants were already longtime residents and were certainly the more glamorous New York ballclub, featuring legendary hurler Christy Mathewson. But the roles began to reverse when the Yankees acquired charismatic power hitter Babe Ruth before the 1920 season. Suddenly, the houseguests were being hailed as kings by an increasingly interested fanbase. Chafing at the reversal, the Giants' management eventually forced the Yankees to build a home of their own. They would, of course, begin construction just across the Harlem River in the Bronx. As the tensions rose behind the scenes, the clubs found themselves facing off on the field, as well.

The 1921 World Series between the Yankees and Giants was remembered for firsts. It was the first to be broadcast on the radio, with sportswriter Grantland Rice behind the microphone. It was also the first to be played exclusively at one stadium. During the Series, Ruth dealt with several injuries. His dramatic mannerisms bred skepticism and a belief that he may have been playing up his maladies. The prideful Bambino threatened to fight any reporter who questioned his toughness, but an infected elbow later kept him from playing in two games as the Giants won the Series in eight games (the current seven-game format wasn't codified until the next year). John McGraw's Giants became the first team to rally from a 2-games-to-none deficit.

In 1922, the teams met again in the Fall Classic, with the Giants sweeping the Yankees in four games, embarrassing them in the process. Ruth lost his focus thanks to constant heckling and a brief scuffle with Giants infielder Johnny Rawlings after Game 3. The Giants' psychological edge and on-field dominance over the Yankees before the 1923 Series left Reds pitcher Eppa Rixey to write, "McGraw is a man without peer in directing a ballclub. His hand was plainly visible in the last two series and it will be evident again this fall, spurring his men on."

Even the fiery McGraw's strategy was no match for the Yankees in the first year of Yankee Stadium's existence. With Ruth making an effort to curtail his famous off-the-field carousing and focus all his energies on the diamond, the Yankees captured the first of the 26 world championships they would win during the stadium's lifespan behind the Sultan of Swat's three home runs.

WORLD SERIES RIVALS

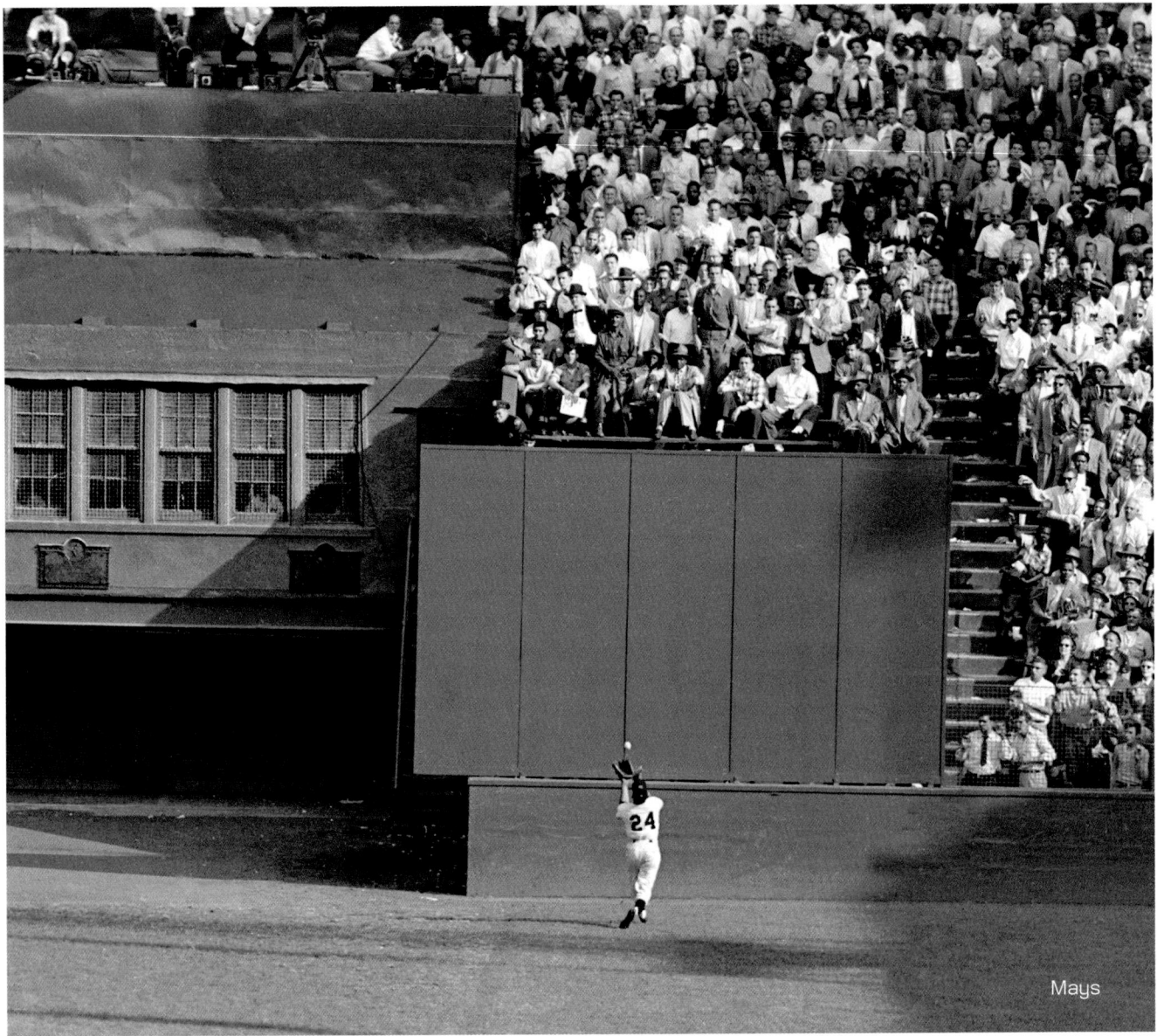

Mays

OVER-THE-SHOULDER UPSET

In 1954, the Cleveland Indians charged through the American League like a runaway freight train. The Tribe was so good that future Hall-of-Fame pitcher Bob Feller was merely a spot starter, as the 35-year-old was overshadowed by staff aces Bob Lemon and Early Wynn. Outfielder Larry Doby led the league in home runs and RBI, and after establishing a new American League single-season record on the second-to-last day of the campaign with their 111th win, the Indians came into the World Series as heavy favorites over the New York Giants.

"Our focus was on beating that [single-season victory] record of the '27 Yankees, and once we got it, we relaxed," Doby admitted years later. "It meant a lot to the [city of Cleveland]. But then, two days later, we're in the World Series. I just don't think we were mentally ready."

The Giants let the Tribe know they meant business late in Game 1 when 23-year-old center fielder Willie Mays tracked down Vic Wertz's 450-foot drive, making the most famous over-the-shoulder catch in the sport's history. "I wasn't lucky to get that one," said Mays 30 years later. "I was with it all the way." Cleveland never recovered, and Dusty Rhodes homered to win the game in 10 innings, setting in motion a surprising sweep.

"To this day I question myself about that one event in my life more than any other. It's something I'll never get over," Indians Manager Al Lopez lamented years later.

CLASH OF THE TITANS

Despite being considered the premier talents in their respective circuits, Ty Cobb and Honus Wagner could not have had less in common. The fiery Cobb dominated the American League until Babe Ruth emerged and ended the Deadball Era. Wagner did the same thing in the National League, winning eight batting titles and five stolen base crowns between the 1900 and 1912 seasons. But while Cobb was viewed as a snarling, mean, dirty player who would do anything to win, even inspiring hatred from his own teammates, Wagner was a gentleman, humble and widely beloved, who had the sport wrapping its arms around him.

In their lone World Series matchup in 1909, Wagner was the proven veteran who outplayed the 22-year-old Cobb. Both were elected into Cooperstown with the Hall of Fame's inaugural class. But in this Series, the Pirates, who played their home games in the modern concrete-and-steel Forbes Field, proved to be the better team, winning in seven games. And Wagner was the better player. He hit .333, going 8 for 24 with six RBI and a record six stolen bases, befitting his nickname of "The Flying Dutchman."

Cobb lost for the third straight time in a championship showdown and didn't do much to distinguish himself along the way. A .377 hitter during the '09 regular season, the "Georgia Peach" batted just .231 in the Series and swiped a mere two bases after stealing 76 that year. Sportswriters began calling Cobb "The Greatest Player Never to Win a Championship" — something that, not surprisingly, irritated the cantankerous Cobb to no end.

Cobb (left), Wagner

TALE OF THE TAPE: WAGNER'S AND COBB'S CAREER STATS									
Player	G	R	H	HR	RBI	SB	AVG	OBP	SLG
Cobb	3,034	2,246	4,189	117	1,938	897	.366	.433	.512
Wagner	2,794	1,739	3,420	101	1,733	723	.328	.391	.467

WORLD SERIES RIVALS

Shibe Park

HISTORY REPEATS ITSELF

When the Athletics and Giants met in Interleague Play for the first time in 1997, the Bay Area neighbors bemoaned the lack of animosity. "From my standpoint, we ought to do everything we can to create that," said Athletics General Manager Sandy Alderson. It was presumed that such a rivalry would develop in the future, as Interleague confrontations would become an annual fixture. Perhaps if Alderson wanted to fuel the nascent rivalry, he should have given his players a history lesson.

Nearly a century earlier, New York Giants Manager John McGraw joked that the Philadelphia Athletics were nothing more than "white elephants." It would soon be clear that he greatly underestimated his rival, A's skipper Connie Mack, even if he got the better of him initially. A rivalry sprouted in 1905, when the Giants and A's met in the World Series just one year after McGraw and Giants Owner John Brush boycotted the Classic because of their belief in the NL's superiority. Christy Mathewson, McGraw's all-time favorite player, pitched three complete-game shutouts in six days to win the '05 Series for New York.

A few years later, the balance of power shifted, and the A's had a glitzier nickname. Eddie Collins, Jack Barry, Frank Baker and Stuffy McInnis combined to form the "$100,000 Infield." With Mack guiding such a talent-laden roster, they were a powerhouse during the 1910s. After a six-day delay due to torrential rainstorms, Athletics pitcher Chief Bender outdueled Mathewson in Game 4, giving the Athletics a 3-games-to-1 Series advantage and setting the stage for their eventual six-game triumph. In 1913, Mack's bunch was even more dominant, with Bender winning twice as the A's finished off the Giants in five games. By this time, fan interest was rabid, with the teams drawing 36,291 fans for the Series opener at the Polo Grounds.

STREETCAR SERIES

The first and last all–St. Louis Fall Classic drew 206,708 fans over six games, which was considered a respectable amount given the capacity of Sportsman's Park, which hosted all the contests. Indicative of the small-town feel of St. Louis was the fact that Billy Southworth and Luke Sewell — the managers for the Cardinals and Browns, respectively, who figured that only one team could ever be home at a time — shared an apartment during the regular season just as the teams shared the ballpark.

Appropriate for a pair of clubs as different as night and day, each one arrived in the 1944 World Series by a very different road. The Cardinals were the standard bearers for the National League, eclipsing 100 wins for the third season in a row. It wasn't until the Baltimore Orioles of 1969–71 that the feat was equaled. The Browns were the American League's latest "Hitless Wonders," trying to claim a championship with a meek offense, in much the same fashion as the 1906 White Sox. They were no match for the Cardinals' pitchers, who struck out 49 batters in six games, including a standout showing by Max Lanier. Future Hall of Famer Stan Musial was expectedly among the Cards' hitting stars.

But in the years since, a debate about the Series has surfaced. Did the Cardinals win it, or did the Browns fumble it away? The Redbirds supported their strong pitching with a crisp showing in the field from star shortstop Marty "Slats" Marion and the defenders around him. They handled all but one chance cleanly. The Browns, in contrast, were uncharacteristically clumsy, effectively killing a Cinderella story that captivated the city when they topped the Detroit Tigers by one game for the American League pennant. Chatterbox second baseman Don Gutteridge and shortstop Vernon Stephens botched a double play in the fourth inning of the final game on George Kurowski's groundball. The throw from Stephens was slightly off line, and Gutteridge made it worse by leaving the bag too soon. The gaffe led to a pair of unearned runs that "was more than the stout-hearted, right-handed pitching of the Browns could take" wrote the United Press.

chapter 8
SHORT-TERM RIVALRIES

Baseball's most fractious rivalries tend to be rooted in both history and proximity, with years of players and fans butting heads. Such teams have been at each other's throats for so long that it doesn't particularly matter if they are both competitive at any given time. Flash rivalries — those that rise up fast and furious — can be just as intense, with animosity bubbling over quickly after even just one memorable confrontation. These disputes generally involve two evenly matched teams going toe to toe for the same prize. They may not have the brand recognition of some other notable pairings, but these short-term feuds usually feature contending teams delivering some of the game's most thrilling moments.

RED ALL OVER

If you ask St. Louis Cardinals Manager Tony La Russa, the reason that opponents don't like his ballclub is because it has won often under his watch. His players, though, have also made it abundantly clear that they too can hold a grudge. Just ask Cincinnati Reds second baseman Brandon Phillips. With both NL Central teams battling in the standings in 2010, the tension rose along with the mercury all summer long.

After the Cardinals complained about slick baseballs and asked the umpires to check the cap of Reds pitcher Bronson Arroyo for illegal substances during a series early in the season, Phillips said, "I really hate the Cardinals. Compared to the Cardinals, I love the Chicago Cubs. Let me make this clear: I *really* hate the Cardinals."

When Phillips led off a game during an August 2010 series and tapped Cardinals' catcher Yadier Molina's shin guard as a friendly gesture, Molina was having none of it. He started jawing with Phillips. Shoving ensued and an ugly, benches-clearing brawl followed. Longtime managerial adversaries La Russa and Dusty Baker argued at the plate as the fight spread to the backstop. During the melee, Cards reserve catcher Jason LaRue sustained a mild concussion from a kick to the head by Reds pitcher Johnny Cueto.

"He talked bad about my team," Molina said of Phillips on Fox Sports Midwest. "Don't talk bad and come up and say 'Hi' to me. That's stupid."

After Cincinnati captured the division in 2010 — the team's first NL Central crown since 1995 — the bad blood continued to flow in 2011, with Reds Hall of Fame broadcaster Marty Brennaman even getting in on the action when he ripped Cardinals ace Chris Carpenter on air for complaining about field conditions during a soggy game. When Reds closer Francisco Cordero hit Cardinals first baseman Albert Pujols with a pitch in a May 2011 game, the Cardinals' bench barked at the closer for plunking their perennial MVP candidate.

"There are times that you beat us — if we're not good enough — but you're never going to scare us, and we're never going to back down," La Russa said.

Phillips (sliding)

SHORT-TERM RIVALRIES

Polo Grounds

A GIANT MISTAKE

The 1908 pennant race between the Chicago Cubs and the New York Giants was shaped by what *Baseball Anecdotes* referred to as the "most famous play in baseball history." On Sept. 23, 1908, the Giants' Al Bridwell hit what appeared to be a game-winning single in the bottom of the ninth, scoring Moose McCormick. The crowd stormed the field at the Polo Grounds as the game appeared to be over, and Fred Merkle, who had been the runner on first, left the base line as McCormick scored.

But the Cubs' Johnny Evers pointed out to umpire Hank O'Day that Merkle never touched second. After some trouble getting the ball back in from the outfield — and some contend it was a different ball altogether — Evers stepped on second to register a force out. The game remained a tie. The Giants exploded. New York ace Christy Mathewson threatened to quit the sport if the decision was upheld. The umpires gathered to discuss a remedy. The scene was so hectic that police escorted the Cubs from the field and the decision wasn't confirmed until the next day.

After the rivals finished the season with identical 98-55 records, it was necessary to replay the game at the end of the season to determine the pennant, and on Oct. 8, the Cubs finally won the game. It's hard for modern fans to accept the Cubs having *good* luck, but even more difficult for the Giants was the demonization of their then 19-year-old first baseman, whose miscue on the basepaths is still remembered as "Merkle's Boner." Said Giants Manager John McGraw, "It's criminal to say that Merkle is stupid and to blame the loss of the pennant on him. He is one of the smartest and best players on this club. ... We were robbed of it and you can't say Merkle did that."

1927 Chicago American Giants

THE OTHER GIANTS

Rube Foster founded the Negro National League in 1920 because he knew that African-American players were every bit as talented as their white counterparts — and also that fans would pay to see them play. Under his guidance, the Chicago American Giants became the dominant team in black baseball, winning titles in 1920, 1921 and '22. When the Giants took the field it was like "seeing the gods come down from heaven," said Buck O'Neil, who would later star for the Kansas City Monarchs.

The Monarchs would eventually develop into the American Giants' most powerful rivals. White businessman J.L. Wilkinson founded the Monarchs, who quickly became a major attraction in the Negro Leagues. The majestic Monarchs won the pennant from 1923–25 and in 1929, and would eventually feature future Big Leaguers like Ernie Banks and Jackie Robinson.

The back-and-forth battling between these teams peaked in 1926, when the Giants won a hotly contested nine-game playoff by sweeping a doubleheader on the season's final day. The Giants would successfully defend their crown in 1927. The skill and popularity of these two teams set the stage for interracial barnstorming tours and, eventually, the sport's integration.

SHORT-TERM RIVALRIES

Bench

A DECADE OF DOMINANCE

During the 1970s, most National League teams felt they had to overcome the powerhouse Cincinnati Reds in order to win the pennant. Well, the Los Angeles Dodgers liked to think that the Reds had to get by *them*. In nine of the decade's 10 years, either the Dodgers or Reds won the NL West, and they combined for seven trips to the Fall Classic.

Although the lack of a Wild Card before 1994 prevented these foes from facing off in the playoffs, they finished one-two in the standings eight times during the decade, including seven straight seasons. Their perennial playoff appearances in the '70s netted two World Series titles, both won by the Reds in consecutive years. Anchored by players like Joe Morgan, Pete Rose and Johnny Bench, the Reds earned every letter of their "Big Red Machine" nickname, outscoring their opponents by a combined total of 478 runs in their 1975 and '76 championship campaigns.

Relying on a strong and deep pitching staff, the Dodgers won 85 or more games every year from 1970–78. Dodgers pitchers led the Senior Circuit in ERA six times, finishing in the top five in that category in all but one year of the decade. With less-heralded stalwarts like Ron Cey, Davey Lopes, Bill Buckner and Don Sutton, the Dodgers did all they could to best their high-profile opponents. Their efforts would ultimately yield a title in 1981, when the rules of the strike-shortened season kept a Reds team with more total wins out of the playoffs.

ORIGINAL BAD BOYS

Nearly a century before the 1980s Detroit Pistons brought a hard-nosed, win-at-all-costs mentality to the NBA, the Baltimore Orioles of the 1890s were playing with a ferocity that bordered on viciousness. While under the leadership of legends John McGraw and Ned Hanlon, *The Sporting News* proclaimed that "The Orioles [were] playing the dirtiest ball ever seen in the country."

They would spike opposing players, grab their belts while attempting to pick them off or to keep them from advancing to the next base, and trip or injure anyone in their path, including umpires. In between the occasional riots, the Boston Beaneaters created a rivalry with the Orioles, which bubbled over during the 1897 NL pennant race. Although the Orioles won 12 straight late in the season, Boston's 22-2 record in June staked it to a half-game lead when the teams met for a three-game series on Sept. 24.

The encounter became the stuff of movie scripts, with the boorish play that had defined the earlier part of the season briefly replaced by cleaner baseball. The series attracted roughly 57,000 fans to Union Park, as many fringe followers delighted in the spectacle. Boston shortstop Herman Long robbed Wee Willie Keeler — who had a 44-game hitting streak that year — of a hit, instead starting a critical double play in Boston's 6-4 win in the opener. Baltimore responded with a 6-3 victory to give itself a chance to take over first place in Monday's finale.

Once more, bats, rather than fists, defined the action. The Orioles rocked Boston's Kid Nichols, but Boston also belted all of Baltimore's hurlers, winning easily, 19-10. Many years later, in his *Historical Baseball Abstract*, Bill James called it "probably the greatest series in nineteenth-century baseball."

SHORT-TERM RIVALRIES

NEW PECKING ORDER

The blockbuster trade in June 1983 that shipped the St. Louis Cardinals' 29-year-old All-Star first baseman Keith Hernandez to the Mets in exchange for pitchers Neil Allen and Rick Ownbey planted the seeds of a 1980s rivalry that was as fierce as any conflict in baseball at the time. Under skipper Whitey Herzog, the Cards were known for playing an up-tempo game relying on aggressive baserunning and athletic defense, and with Hernandez's Gold Glove play at first base, they had just won the 1982 World Series.

When Hernandez arrived in Queens, he joined a struggling team without an identity. But by 1985, the club had molded itself in the image of its hardworking new leader. The continued progression of talented youngsters Dwight Gooden and Darryl Strawberry also helped the team lift itself up from the second division.

Allen, the former Met, surrendered a game-winning homer to New York catcher Gary Carter on Opening Day. The teams traded jabs all summer long before the Cardinals eventually eliminated the Mets from the playoff race in the last week of the season. St. Louis would go on to reach the World Series as the Mets simmered during the Hot Stove season.

New York's perpetually dirt-stained rookie outfielder, Lenny Dykstra, bitter at being bumped from playoff contention, began using an expletive when referring to the Cardinals. Early into the 1986 season, the Mets exacted revenge when they went into Busch Stadium and swept a four-game series in April. The Mets outscored St. Louis, 23-10, during the sweep, which included a dominant shutout by Gooden. With Hernandez firmly entrenched as the clubhouse leader, the Mets rolled to a franchise-best 108 wins that season. The Mets took 12 of 18 from the Cards and unseated them as NL champions, winning the division by more than 20 games and storming to their own World Series crown.

HERNANDEZ'S STATS WITH THE CARDINALS AND METS						
Team	G	R	H	RBI	AVG	Gold Gloves
Cardinals	1,165	662	1,217	595	.299	5
Mets	880	455	939	468	.297	6

Hernandez

SHORT-TERM RIVALRIES

STRONG-ARM TACTICS

Entering the 1998 season, it remained unclear whether it was the New York Yankees or Baltimore Orioles who were about to gain control of the AL East. Although New York had captured the 1996 World Series with a hardworking group of players, including rookie shortstop Derek Jeter, the gritty team from Charm City had claimed the division crown with 98 wins in 1997, en route to appearing in the ALCS for the second straight year.

With a solid pitching rotation led by Mike Mussina, Scott Erickson and Jimmy Key, and a lineup that included established players like Cal Ripken Jr., Roberto Alomar, Rafael Palmeiro and Brady Anderson, the Orioles fielded a veteran lineup in 1998. With the bitter tastes of ALCS defeats in '96 and '97 still fresh, they were as determined as ever to reach the promised land. After opening the '98 season on a 10-2 tear, the Birds scuffled through the second half of April and the first few weeks of May. They arrived at Yankee Stadium on May 19 having dropped seven of their last nine games. With the Yankees' division lead expanding, the pressure was on Baltimore.

While the Orioles' bats staked closer Armando Benitez to a 5-3 lead, the pressure proved too much. After surrendering a go-ahead, three-run home run to Bernie Williams, Benitez drilled Yankees first baseman Tino Martinez with a fastball in the back. The pitch seemed a clear act of retaliation, and the benches emptied.

When the teams met again that season, Orioles Manager Ray Miller didn't pitch Benitez, despite his being available after an eight-game suspension. The 25-year-old Benitez, who was distraught over his actions, said he sent Martinez a written apology three days after the incident, but Martinez never confirmed receiving it.

Although Martinez fell into a deep slump after getting plunked, the Yankees as a team did not. They coalesced into one of the era's most powerful forces. The dominant '98 Yankees finished the regular season with 114 wins and stormed through the postseason to claim another World Series title. Joe Torre's Bombers would capture the championship again in 1999 and 2000 — when they beat Benitez's Mets — and win another pair of pennants in 2001 and 2003.

Alomar (jumping)

SHORT-TERM RIVALRIES

Back row (left to right): Plank, Quinn, Walker, Schreckengost, Waddell, Davis, Monte Cross, Fultz. Center row: Powers, Seybold, Lave Cross, Connie Mack, Murphy, Castro, Mitchell. Front row: Hastings, Hartsel, Wilson.

BATTLE FOR PHILADELPHIA

For years, the National League was considered the country's premier professional baseball circuit. While other leagues would surface and struggle to compete, they couldn't meet either the revenue or the standard of play of the NL. Prominent among those minor leagues was the Western League. While the owners of NL clubs hoped it would go the way of so many upstarts that came before it, Western League President Byron "Ban" Johnson forged the American League from the former's remnants during a meeting with fellow owners in a Chicago hotel.

Johnson wasn't interested in inferior status. He tried to win the public relations battle by juxtaposing the AL's "clean" style with the rough-and-tumble play of the NL. He brashly placed AL teams in established NL cities and even tried to entice some star players into switching leagues.

Philadelphia soon became the epicenter for the fight between the leagues. The Phillies were the city's longstanding National League team. To compete, the AL founded the Philadelphia Athletics, managed ultimately by the "dean" of baseball, Connie Mack. Mack lured away Phillies hitting sensation Nap Lajoie, but the Phillies took legal action, getting a court injunction to prevent Lajoie from playing any home games during his one campaign playing for the Quaker City's AL representative. Rather than give in and surrender Lajoie, Mack traded him to another AL club in Cleveland, solving the problem. The franchise in Cleveland was so delighted it briefly changed its nickname to the Naps. On the field, the Athletics settled the argument even further with the Phillies.

Under Mack's leadership, a team that was derisively named the "white elephants" by Giants Manager John McGraw won the 1902 AL pennant. Led by pitcher Rube Waddell's 24 wins, the Athletics won 83 games to the Phillies' 56 that year. The Athletics drew a league-best 420,078 fans, while the Phillies' 112,066 total was the worst in the NL. Only two teams in either league had a winning percentage better than the Athletics over the decade, their superiority going a long way toward legitimizing the fledgling American League.

CHIP OFF THE OLD BLOCK

After being groomed by his father to be the next Mickey Mantle, Chipper Jones made quite a name for himself in New York City without ever donning Yankees pinstripes. As a star third baseman for the Atlanta Braves, Jones tormented the Mets in one of the hottest rivalries of the 1990s and early 2000s.

Beginning in 1995, Jones played 88 career games at Shea Stadium in Queens and was unstoppable there. He hit .313 with 19 home runs and 55 RBI. Halfway through the 2011 season, nearly three years after Shea closed, those numbers remained his most impressive body of work in any opposing stadium.

"This atmosphere is what gets you geeked up to play here. The fans being so loyal and so — just crazy," Jones said.

Mets fans — and pitchers — went all out trying to unnerve the switch hitter. In 1999, fans chanted "La-rry! La-rry!" when they learned that Jones didn't care for his given name. Nothing worked. Jones locked up NL MVP honors that season, the final push coming when he clubbed four home runs in a late three-game sweep of the Mets. In the playoffs, the Mets wisely pitched around Jones, leaving little to chance.

A licensed Mets killer by 2004, Jones provided a novel tribute to his rival's home. On Aug. 30, the All-Star named his newborn son Shea in honor of the stadium of his longtime rival.

"I love that place," said Jones when asked why he did such a thing. "Check the numbers." Before Shea Stadium was torn down following the 2008 season, Jones bought a pair of seats for $869 as a keepsake.

Jones

SHORT-TERM RIVALRIES

PENNSYLVANIA POWER STRUGGLE

Long before the Phillies traded barbs with the Mets in 2007, they staged a decade-long battle for NL East supremacy with the Pittsburgh Pirates. In the years after the 1969 realignment, when both leagues adopted a total of four divisions, the Pirates and Phillies were regularly vying for the same playoff spot.

Led by Willie Stargell and Dave Parker, the Pirates won two World Series during the 1970s, reached the National League Championship Series six times and were perennially in contention. Those '70s Pirates were an eclectic but formidable bunch.

The Phillies had the finest farm system in the 1970s, which groomed youngsters to play alongside stars like third baseman Mike Schmidt and pitcher Steve Carlton. From 1975–79, Philadelphia averaged 92 wins and won the division three times, losing in the NLCS on each occasion. While some rivalries can generate an outright dislike between the teams involved, this Keystone battle was fascinating for the mutual respect that developed instead. In 1978, the Phillies topped the Pirates by 1.5 games for the NL East crown. The reaction afterward spoke volumes, as several Phillies stopped by the Pirates' clubhouse after the clinching victory.

"Your guys scared the life out of us. They never quit," scrappy shortstop Larry Bowa said.

Responded Bucs Manager Chuck Tanner, after being given some champagne by Phils pitcher Jim Kaat, "You guys didn't either. That's what this is all about, isn't it?"

The Pirates rebounded in 1979 with the "We Are Family" crew, winning the World Series. The Phillies, appropriately, won the title in 1980, capping more than a decade of bare-fisted Pennsylvania confrontations with championship rings on both sides.

Stargell

SHORT-TERM RIVALRIES

Dolph Camilli (sliding)

HOME-FRONT HEROICS

During the 1940s, every close pennant race in the National League, save for one, featured the Dodgers and Cardinals. The pair finished in the top two spots five times, and the Cards nabbed a top two finish in four other years. While Brooklyn stormed to a few brilliant campaigns, it was the Cardinals who were the most consistent team of the decade, running up a cumulative 960-580 record.

Long viewed as misfits and eccentrics, the Dodgers were finally transformed into contenders in 1939, one year after Larry MacPhail took over the front office. He named Leo "the Lip" Durocher as field manager. In 1941, the Dodgers captured their first pennant in 21 years, edging the Cardinals by 2.5 games. That Dodgers club won 100 games and sported a winning record against all but one NL club, splitting the season series with St. Louis, 11-11. With Hall of Famers Billy Herman, Pee Wee Reese and Joe Medwick on the squad, that '41 Brooklyn side hoped to stake a claim to being one of the greatest ever, but it dropped the Fall Classic to the Yankees. Determined to avenge its Series loss, the Dodgers were even better in 1942, reeling off 104 wins. The only problem was that the Cardinals won an astounding 106 games. The 13-9 season series advantage for St. Louis accounted for the difference in the standings.

By 1946, the Cardinals had become known more for their pitching, while the Dodgers sported a well-rounded lineup. Durocher was considered to have his best year as a manager, whipping a young club into contending shape. Yet he still couldn't eclipse the Cardinals. Durocher did his best to unnerve them, predicting that the Cards would crack in September. But the Cardinals did not limp into the playoffs, instead going 16-8 against Brooklyn during the season and winning the World Series, silencing the Lip.

SHORT-TERM RIVALRIES

Bell

BORDER WAR

Detroit Manager Sparky Anderson would tell anyone who would listen that his 1987 Tigers were better than his world champion '84 club — the one that had steamrolled through the American League and then routed the San Diego Padres to capture the title. It was hard to take him seriously when the club sat 11 games back in the division on May 5.

Even when the Tigers were knee-deep in the playoff race come mid-July, few figured they could catch the Blue Jays, winners of the division title in 1985. Toronto's offense was fueled by the bat of slugging outfielder George Bell, who became the first native of the Dominican Republic to win the AL MVP Award. As good as he was — .308 average, 47 home runs, 134 RBI — he couldn't prevent the team's historic nosedive. The Blue Jays finished with seven straight losses, rivaling the 1964 Phillies for one of the worst collapses ever. The Tigers, meanwhile, were just catching their second wind down the stretch. Led by their own MVP hopeful, Alan Trammell — .343 average, 28 home runs, 105 RBI — and his double play–partner Lou Whitaker, Detroit won five of its final six games. Doyle Alexander, acquired in August in a trade with Atlanta — in exchange for pitching prospect John Smoltz — won all nine of his decisions, and Frank Tanana shut out Toronto, 1-0, with a six-hitter to clinch the division.

"This was nicer than '84," said Tigers first baseman Dave Bergman. "In '84, things seemed to go our way all year long. This was a roller-coaster year. Everyone stuck together, pulled for one another and picked each other up. And at the end, the experience paid off."

"Obviously people are going to say, 'You blew it, you choked.' There will be a lot of negative things said," added defiant Jays third baseman Rance Mulliniks. "But the people who are going to say that have never been in this situation."

Toronto soothed lingering wounds from its 1987 riches-to-gags story by winning back-to-back World Series titles in the early 1990s.

Trammell

Thomson

chapter 9
DODGERS-GIANTS

Although the Yankees and Dodgers have squared off in several memorable World Series, that fall matchup isn't the marquee rivalry for either team. The Yankees save their best efforts for the Red Sox, while the Dodgers have a rival that they've battled for more than a century, on one coast and then another. The Dodgers and Giants tangled all season long in the early days of the National League, back when both were residents of the Empire State. "In Brooklyn, 'Giant' is the dirtiest word in the language," legendary sportswriter Red Smith wrote. Counted among the indelible moments in this historic pairing is Bobby Thomson's "Shot Heard 'Round the World" in 1951. Several years after that famous home run, both clubs would take their rivalry to the Pacific Coast. Although the Majors may have been new to California, local fans were able to enjoy one of the game's most historic rivalries.

'THE SHOT HEARD 'ROUND THE WORLD'

When a shutout loss to the Phillies at the Polo Grounds cut the New York Giants' deficit in the NL standings to 13 games on Aug. 11, 1951, it seemed a lock that the club's 14-season playoff drought would continue. Yet a sweep of a doubleheader the next day began an unexpected 16-game winning streak that brought the Giants back into the thick of the pennant race.

By posting a 20-5 mark in September, Leo Durocher's Giants forced a three-game playoff with the Brooklyn Dodgers for the pennant. *The New York Times* wrote, "For the next few days even the grimmest of world-wide news will have an overshadowing rival for attention in the whirl and clash of the great American game."

The Giants won the first game, 3-1, but the Dodgers pounded Giants spot starter Sheldon Jones, 10-0, to even the series. In the winner-take-all finale, Dodgers ace Don Newcombe was dominant and the Dodgers led, 4-1, in the ninth inning. It appeared "Newk" had restored order to a season that his team had seemingly all but sewn up weeks earlier. But the Giants had a secret.

In 2001, the *Wall Street Journal* revealed that the New York club had used a sign-stealing system during the '51 season to tip pitches to hitters. A Giants coach hid in the Polo Grounds' center-field clubhouse armed with a Wollensak telescope, stealing the catcher's signs and relaying them to the dugout with a bell and buzzer. Bobby Thomson, who lost his starting center field job to rookie Willie Mays that year, wouldn't admit that he knew what was coming when he stepped into the box with two men on in the bottom of the ninth.

Newcombe was gone after allowing a run, and Ralph Branca, who gave up a homer to Thomson in the series opener, stood on the mound. The Giants figured Branca would walk Thomson to pitch to the slumping Mays. Instead, Branca fired home a first-pitch fastball for a strike. Thomson watched the pitch all the way because, as he later admitted, "I was so nervous my eyeballs were vibrating." Catcher Rube Walker called for another fastball and Branca followed orders, sending home a high-and-tight heater. Thomson pulled it over the left-field fence, setting off delirium as broadcaster Russ Hodges delivered the distinctive call: "It's a long drive. It's gonna be … I believe … the Giants win the pennant! The Giants win the pennant!"

DODGERS-GIANTS

FINLEY'S GRAND CLINCHER

Even for Hollywood, this script was a bit corny, but baseball fans are less critical of plot twists than movie reviewers. When the Dodgers acquired well-traveled veteran outfielder Steve Finley from the Diamondbacks in July 2004, there was no doubt that his best days were behind him. But the new arrival felt comfortable in the NL West and appreciated that Dodgers Manager Jim Tracy graciously gave him his uniform No. 12. In spite of that, the 39-year-old hadn't done much to help the club entering the second-to-last day of the season, when the Dodgers were hosting the Giants and looking to lock up the division crown. But like many older athletes, Finley insisted he could still contribute.

"I visualized it happening. I was so relaxed heading up to the plate," Finley would say years later. The Dodgers trailed, 3-0, entering the ninth inning, but the San Francisco bullpen quickly collapsed. Giants closer Dustin Hermanson allowed a single to Shawn Green before walking three batters to force in a run. Shortstop Cody Ransom then botched a ground ball as another run scored. After Jayson Werth singled home the tying run, beleaguered Giants Manager Felipe Alou turned to left-hander Wayne Franklin. Tracy responded with Finley, who had singled earlier.

"I wanted this situation," Finley said. "I wanted to get the hit."

Finley crushed Franklin's pitch over the same right-field fence that Kirk Gibson cleared with his dramatic walk-off homer in Game 1 of the 1988 World Series. "You just can't believe how it felt," said a floored Tracy. It's one thing to clinch a playoff berth. But to do so in jaw-dropping fashion against a hated rival, it doesn't get much better than that.

Or in the case of the Giants, much more bitter. "You just walk off, and you just try to move on," Franklin said.

Wills

Morgan

PROMOTION FOR A PENNANT

Not much was expected of the Dodgers in 1959. The sentiment seemed to be affirmed as they scuffled through the first two months of the season around the .500 mark, never getting closer than a handful of games to the top of the standings. Perhaps looking toward the future, though, the Dodgers made a decision in early June that drastically improved their present: They promoted 26-year-old shortstop Maury Wills.

With Wills infusing energy into the club, the Dodgers began chasing down the Giants, pulling within two games with eight to go. The Giants were still slim favorites, if only because the final series between the clubs would be held at Seals Stadium in San Francisco. Heading into that three-game series in September, there had already been talk that the Giants would become the first California-based team to win the World Series. Instead, the Dodgers raced past them, sweeping their northern neighbor behind the arms of Roger Craig, Don Drysdale and Johnny Podres. It was a convincing beatdown, with the Dodgers outscoring the Giants, 17-6, with Wills going 7 for 13. The Giants, meanwhile, were fracturing on the field and in the clubhouse. After finishing in third place, Giants star Orlando Cepeda lashed out at Manager Bill Rigney. "He lost the pennant for us. He can't manage; he doesn't know baseball or baseball players."

MORGAN'S KNOCKOUT SWING

Led by veteran outfielders Dusty Baker and Pedro Guerrero, the 1982 Dodgers entered the last weekend of the season intent on clinching a playoff spot. Mired in a dogfight with the Atlanta Braves for the NL West crown, the Dodgers looked to their top three starters — Jerry Reuss, Bob Welch and Fernando Valenzuela — to lead the charge when they went up to Candlestick Park for the final three games against San Francisco. Behind Reuss and Welch, the Dodgers won the first two contests, thus eliminating the Giants with one game left. But Los Angeles still needed one more victory on the final day to match Atlanta.

On the 31st anniversary of Bobby Thomson's "Shot Heard 'Round the World," the clubs added yet another chapter to their storied rivalry. Giants second baseman Joe Morgan played the role of Thomson while Dodgers southpaw Terry Forster stood in on the mound for pitcher Ralph Branca. Morgan was enjoying a solid season in the twilight of his career, but he had never been known as a home run hitter. Having allowed just eight homers to a lefty in his near decade-long stint in the Bigs, Forster threw a hanging slider that Morgan crushed. The Dodgers' playoff dreams vanished into the sky with the ball. As it cleared the fence, the pitcher fired his glove in disgust.

"The worst moment of my career," said Forster. It was payback for the Giants.

"I know the feeling the Dodgers have right now. They can't believe what's happening to them," Morgan said. "I put my A-1 No. 1 swing on it."

DODGERS-GIANTS

Hershiser

TALE OF THE TAPE: DRYSDALE'S AND HERSHISER'S SCORELESS STREAKS								
Player	W	ERA	IP	H	R	BB	SO	WHIP
Drysdale	7	0.00	58.2	30	0	10	46	0.686
Hershiser	6	0.00	60	33	0	12	39	0.750

NOTHING BUT ZEROES

Mention Don Drysdale and Orel Hershiser to even the casual baseball fan, and they'll likely muse about their historic scoreless inning streaks. Drop their names to San Francisco fans, and their focus is less on zeroes and more on Giant controversies.

In 1968, Don Drysdale was the Los Agneles Dodgers' answer to Bob Gibson in the "Year of the Pitcher." The 6-foot-5 right-hander was closing in on the Major League record for most consecutive scoreless innings when he faced the Giants on May 31. In the ninth, San Francisco had loaded the bases with none out, and Drysdale threw an inside pitch that hit Dick Dietz. Streak over? Not so fast. The umpire ruled the pitch a ball, saying that Dietz made no attempt to get out of the way. Willie McCovey stayed on third base and Dietz remained at the dish. Drysdale induced a fly out and then retired the final two hitters, notching his fifth straight shutout and running his then-record scoreless streak to 45 innings.

Twenty years later, another Dodgers ace took aim at Drysdale's total of 58.2 scoreless frames. Hershiser's streak got underway in Montreal and gained momentum as he mowed down Atlanta, Cincinnati, Houston, San Francisco and, ultimately, San Diego. This Giant game also sticks out because the streak appeared halted, if not for an umpire's ruling.

In the third inning of his Sept. 23 outing against the Giants, Hershiser ran into trouble. Ernest Riles hit a one-out groundball that appeared to score a run, ending the streak at 43 frames. Instead, the umpire ruled that Giants baserunner Brett Butler interfered with Dodgers shortstop Alfredo Griffin as he tried to turn a double play, meaning both runners were out. Hershiser marched on, ultimately breaking the record with 60 scoreless innings. He wanted to come out in the last game so that he could share the record with Drysdale, but Dodgers Manager Tommy Lasorda wouldn't let him.

"People said it would never be approached, but I knew it would," Drysdale said.

Drysdale

DODGERS-GIANTS

AT A LOSS FOR WORDS ...

Professional ballplayers tend to become proficient at talking to reporters after games regardless of the score. The quotes may be cliched and perfunctory, but they are usually delivered promptly after the final out. That it took the choked-up members of the 1962 Dodgers 56 minutes to compose themselves before they opened the clubhouse doors to reporters following their collapse in the finale of a three-game playoff shows how gut-wrenching and unexpected the loss must have been.

Losing to the Giants is tough enough, but holding a two-run lead with one out in the ninth and watching it disappear left many of the red-eyed Dodgers inconsolable.

"Gentlemen, I just don't feel like talking," the Dodgers' Maury Wills, who stole three bases in the finale to finish the season with 104, told the assembled reporters.

With reliever Ed Roebuck on the hill for Los Angeles, the Giants' final salvo began innocently enough. Roebuck gave up a single to Matty Alou, then recorded the first out. With one out and one on, the right-hander loaded the bases with walks to Willie McCovey and Felipe Alou. Willie Mays stepped into the box. Coming off a stellar season during which he hit a league-leading 49 homers and drove in 141 runs, Mays lined a single off Roebuck's glove, shaving the deficit to 4-3. The struggling pitcher was pulled for Stan Williams, who couldn't stop the bleeding or keep his pitches in the strike zone. A sacrifice fly tied the score, and with bases soon loaded again on an intentional walk, Williams wilted against the Giants' Jim Davenport. He fell behind in the count, 3-1, then missed the zone once again, ushering in the go-ahead run with yet another a free pass.

Unlike 1951's walk-off heroics at the Polo Grounds, the Giants had to record the final three outs as visitors at Dodger Stadium. San Francisco pitcher Billy Pierce did it with ease, leaving the Dodgers heartbroken and the Giants exultant.

"We must have been counted out 50 times this season," Giants Manager Alvin Dark said before his team met and eventually lost to the Yankees in the World Series. "But we always come back."

DODGERS-GIANTS

OUT OF THE BLUE

On paper, the 1965 Dodgers certainly didn't look like one of the franchise's powerhouse teams of the 1940s and '50s. The batting order had question marks from top to bottom and the pitching corps looked like a *MASH* unit. Ace left-hander Sandy Koufax began the season with an arthritic left elbow. Battle-tested Johnny Podres was little help in the rotation. Lou Johnson, who spent a career in the bushes, became the everyday left fielder.

The Associated Press noted that Dodgers Manager Walt Alston, "skilled in handling men and no doubt aided by yards of baling wire, surgical tape and prayer, kept the team up or near the top throughout the long summer months."

Even then, it took a magical finish for the Dodgers to catch their northern rivals. The Giants won 14 games in a row at one point, riding the bat of future Hall of Famer Willie Mays, who finished with 52 home runs and 112 RBI. Leading by two games with 20 to play, Giants skipper Herman Franks did some math and figured that if his club went 12-8 over the final month, then it would advance to the World Series. Beginning on Sept. 16, when critics were still chiding the Los Angeles lineup as being weaker than the hapless New York Mets, the Dodgers reeled off a streak of 15 wins in 16 games to capture the flag by two games.

"We didn't blow it," Franks said. "The Dodgers won it."

Koufax and Don Drysdale anchored the pitching staff, making that weak offense a moot point. The Dodgers took over first place during the last week of the season and clinched the West when they topped the Milwaukee Braves, 3-1, on the penultimate day of the season.

"I have never been on a more determined ballclub," Drysdale said.

KOUFAX'S STATS FROM 1963-66

W-L	ERA	G	IP	BB	SO	WHIP	Cy Young Awards
97-27	1.86	153	1,192.2	259	1,228	0.909	3

Drysdale (left), Koufax

DODGERS-GIANTS

Elster

ELSTER'S EXPLOSION

When the Giants opened their picturesque new ballpark in 2000, no bit of fanfare was left out of the festivities. A squadron of Navy fighter jets performed a flyover. Bobby McFerrin — of "Don't Worry, Be Happy" fame — sang a stirring rendition of the national anthem. A sellout crowd filled the seats for the christening of Pacific Bell Park, the Giants' new jewel of a stadium. Nothing could ruin this day.

Well, almost nothing. With three swings of the bat, Dodgers shortstop Kevin Elster did plenty to steal the spotlight during the opening of the Giants' palace on the water. Most of the memorable performances in this rivalry came from legends like Sandy Koufax or franchise stalwarts like Bobby Thomson. Elster, on the other hand, hadn't even played in the Big Leagues the previous season and was appearing in just his fifth game for the Dodgers. By 2000, he was a veteran vagabond, a non-roster invitee to the Dodgers' Spring Training camp at Vero Beach, Fla. He would play in just 80 games that season and retire immediately after, but he homered three times, all of which were needed to overcome the longballs by Barry Bonds, J.T. Snow and Doug Mirabelli to spoil that day in San Francisco and endear him to Dodgers fans forever.

Marichal (with bat), Roseboro (center) and Koufax

GOING DOWN SWINGING

Best known for a sweeping motion with a high leg kick, Giants pitcher Juan Marichal was the unlikely instigator of one of baseball's ugliest brawls. In the midst of what was becoming a fascinating 1965 pennant race, Marichal faced Dodgers lefty Sandy Koufax in a tight pitchers' duel on Aug. 22. Marichal fired brushback pitches that knocked down Maury Wills and Ron Fairly, and Dodgers catcher John Roseboro wanted Koufax to retaliate. Koufax refused, so Roseboro took action.

With Marichal batting in the third, Roseboro twice threw baseballs back to Koufax that clipped Marichal's ear. Furious, Marichal turned and clubbed Roseboro with his bat before charging the mound. His bat opened up a gash on Roseboro's head that required 14 stitches. Marichal was suspended eight games and fined $1,750. He struggled to regain his consistency after his return that season, especially in visiting parks.

Perhaps more revealing of the true character of the players involved was that Marichal and Roseboro became friends later. When Marichal played for the Dodgers during the 1975 season, it was Roseboro who appealed to fans in Los Angeles to accept him as a member of the team. Marichal admitted that he befriended Roseboro because he wanted Dodgers fans to know the kind of person he really was. Roseboro realized that the brawl was completely out of character for the pitcher.

"There were no hard feelings on my part, and I thought if that was made public, people would believe it was really over with," Roseboro said. "Hey, over the years, you learn to forget things."

DODGERS-GIANTS

Johnson

JOHNSON TURNS THE TIDE

In 1997, the San Francisco Giants were bolstered at the July trading deadline by imports from a pair of AL Central teams that felt they were better off rebuilding than trying to chase a powerful Indians club. The Chicago White Sox sent a trio of pitchers — Wilson Alvarez, Danny Darwin and Roberto Hernandez — to San Francisco, which also acquired little-known catcher Brian Johnson from the Detroit Tigers. The pickups gave the Giants an emotional and physical boost and showed how no division race is entirely isolated from another.

Trailing by two games in the NL West standings in the middle of September, the Giants began a two-game series with the Dodgers at Candlestick Park. After winning the first game, 2-1, the Giants had a chance to pull even with just nine games remaining. With his new club's season hanging in the balance, Johnson hit a solo walk-off homer off reliever Mark Guthrie in the 12th for a 6-5 Giants victory. When Johnson's blast cleared the fence, the Giants were tied for first place. For Johnson, that one swing became the defining moment of a modest career (.248 career average for six different teams over eight seasons).

"It's not too many times in your life when you get to bond with people like that," Johnson said.

Johnson's teammates mobbed him at the plate. Slugger Barry Bonds joyfully raised Giants Manager Dusty Baker onto his shoulders, and the crowd of more than 50,000 exploded with delight as if it was watching a historic scene at the Polo Grounds. This particular shot, though it didn't win the division outright, conjured up images of the magical Giants seasons of 1951 and 1962.

"That was some of the best partying ever seen at this park," Baker said. "It was awesome. That was classic Dodgers–Giants."

After that game, the Dodgers were emotionally spent, and they never recovered, winning just four times over their final nine games. Buoyed by Johnson's blast, though, the Giants went 6-3 down the stretch to clinch a playoff berth.

DODGERS-GIANTS

BONDS BUMPS BIG MAC

Dodgers Manager Jim Tracy could have played the percentages, which, in 2001, meant *not* throwing a strike to Giants slugger Barry Bonds. With his team looking to finish strong, Tracy could have rationalized not pitching to Bonds in the final weekend of the season. But the Dodgers weren't going to reach the playoffs, so Tracy made an important decision. With Bonds sitting on 70 home runs, tied with Mark McGwire for the all-time single-season record, Tracy announced that he wouldn't intentionally walk Bonds just to prevent him from making history at the Dodgers' expense during the three-game series.

"We will go after him," Tracy said. "There's an integrity part of this game, in my mind, that you cannot ignore. And that integrity portion of it, to me, goes far beyond the Giants–Dodgers rivalry."

In the first inning of the series opener, Dodgers pitcher Chan Ho Park, dealing with an achy back, tried to sneak a 1-0 fastball by the left-handed slugger. Bonds launched it an estimated 442 feet into the right-center-field stands for No. 71. He wasn't done, either. He added No. 72 when he led off the third inning with Park still on the hill. Although the Dodgers had been irked when the Giants stopped a game earlier in the season to commemorate Bonds' 500th career home run, Park and his teammates dutifully kept at it despite the fanfare.

After getting just one pinch-hit at-bat in the second game of the series, Bonds launched his historic 73rd home run on the final day of the season. Willie Mays, the outfielder's godfather and owner of 660 career home runs himself, was taken aback by Bonds' feat.

"I am the one he made a liar out of, because I didn't think he would do it," said the Giants' elder statesman.

As the crowd chanted Bonds' name, he gave a short speech before being overcome with emotion.

"We've come a long way. We've had our ups and downs. Thank you," Bonds said.

Bonds

DODGERS-GIANTS

Mike Piazza (left), Tim Wallach

BLUE-HOT SPOTLIGHT

By the end of the 1993 season, the hissing match between the Dodgers and Giants had gone on for decades. They relished spoiling each other's success just as much as achieving their own. Stealing from Joe Morgan's 1982 Giants script, the Dodgers exacted revenge in 1993, leaving one of the best Giants teams ever to watch the playoffs at home on television.

The Giants came to Chavez Ravine during the final weekend of the season just one game behind the Atlanta Braves in the NL West. San Francisco won the first three games of the four-game set and was tied for the division lead with 103 wins entering Sunday. But the Giants' pitching rotation was out of sync, and, on the biggest day of the season, first-year skipper Dusty Baker trotted out struggling 21-year-old rookie Salomon Torres, who had begun the season in Double-A. He had been good in spurts, but was admittedly not ready for this type of pressure.

"We didn't have a lot of options," closer Rod Beck said.

Torres was a wreck, wilting in the spotlight. He lasted just 3.1 innings, allowing three runs on five hits and five walks. The Dodgers grabbed a 2-0 lead in the third inning, coasting to a 12-1 win behind Kevin Gross's complete game.

Torres claimed that he had forgotten about the outing the next day. Giants fans still haven't forgotten, though the advent of the Wild Card in 1994 and a World Series title in 2010 has helped them forgive.

SWITCHING SIDES

Dodgers icon Jackie Robinson was already thinking of his future before a trade made him a potential traitor. In the winter of 1956, the Dodgers shipped Robinson to the rival Giants in exchange for pitcher Dick Littlefield and $30,000.

A few weeks later, Robinson announced in an exclusive with *Look* magazine that he was retiring. The idea that Robinson would hang up his cleats before wearing orange and black makes for great copy, but the reality is that Robinson had intended to quit even before the Giants acquired him.

"I hope [Brooklyn] can win again, unless the Giants win it," said Robinson, trying to be diplomatic.

Having first begun his professional career in 1945 in the Negro Leagues, Robinson was ready to start a life outside of baseball, working in the restaurant business. Ironically, the comments made by Dodgers General Manager Buzzy Bavasi — he accused the future Hall of Famer of duping reporters — only hardened Robinson's resolve to walk away from the game.

"I won't play again for a million dollars," Robinson said.

Robinson

SOURCE NOTES

CHAPTER 1

9. "Yankee Stadium history." Anderson, Dave. "A Yankee Stadium Rivalry Down to its last Out." *The New York Times*. 28 Aug. 2008.

11. "Background on Red Sox trades" Madden, Bill. "Curse Has Gotten Worse; It goes Beyond The Babe." New York *Daily News*. 14 Oct. 1999.

12. "Wade Boggs on going horseback." Curry, Jack. "Boggs Takes a Ride." *The New York Times*. 27 Oct. 1996.

14. "Background on Joe McCarthy." "O'Neill succeeds Ailing Joe." The Associated Press. 24 June 1950.

15. "Yankee Stadium history." Anderson, Dave. "A Yankee Stadium Rivalry Down to its last Out." *New York Times*. 28 Aug. 2008.

16. "Summer of 1941 memories." Anderson, Dave. "For Ted, The Eyes had it." *The New York Times*. 6 July 2002.

17. "Background on Carlton Fisk-Thurman Munson feud." Published at BaseballLibrary.com.

18. "Zimmer on the Boston Massacre." "Zimmer Doesn't Have Fond Memories of '78" Published at AssociatedPress.com. 21 Aug. 2006.

20. "Bucky Dent on his home run." "Dent returns to site of famous homer." The Associated Press. 21 May 2003.

21. "Professors on Ortiz's jersey burial" Robinson, Joshua. "Voodoo Logic: So Who Cursed Whom with Jersey?" *The New York Times*. 17 April 2008.

23. "Yankee Stadium history." Anderson, Dave. "A Yankee Stadium Rivalry Down to its last Out." *The New York Times*. 28 Aug. 2008.

25. "Pedro vs. Roger" Curry, Jack. "Martinez has several ghosts to defeat." *The New York Times*. 16 Oct. 1999.

27. "Aaron Boone on his game-winning home run." MLB Network. 13 May 2011.

28. "Dave Roberts on his famous stolen base." Krasner, Steven and Manza Young, Shalise. "Roberts Returns to Site of Stolen Base." *Providence Journal*. 16 June 2007.

29. "Curt Schilling on the bloody sock game." Schwarz, Alan. "Schilling: I felt like something special was happening." Published at ESPN.com. 26 April 2007.

31. "Talk of the rivalry's origins." Anderson, Dave. "Yankees and Red Sox do the Old 1-2" *The New York Times*. 23 Sept. 2004.

CHAPTER 2

32. "Background on Leo Durocher." "Most of all, Barber was a nice guy: Baseball mourns passing of a pioneer." *San Jose Mercury News*. 23 Oct. 1992.

32. "The Passing of Leo Durocher." Thomas, Rogers. "Leo Durocher, Fiery ex-Manager dies at 86." *The New York Times*. 8 Oct. 1991.

35. "Jimmy Rollins on the Mets." Rubin, Roger. "Jimmy Rollins laughs last as Phillies win East." New York *Daily News*. 1 Oct. 2007.

35. "Phillies-Mets spats." Zolecki, Todd. "Phillies, Mets continue to trade barbs." Published at MLB.com. 18 Feb. 2009.

36. "Background on the Elephant." Davis, Craig. "Search For New Logo Leads to an Old Trunk." *Sun-Sentinel*. 2 Oct. 1988.

36. "Looking back at Connie Mack." "Connie Mack in a Nutshell." United Press International. 19 Oct. 1950.

37. "Background on David Cone." Hagen, Paul. "Cone ends up eating his words." *Los Angeles Times*. 8 Oct. 1988.

37. "Background on Cone-troversy" "Dodgers have the last laugh on Cone." The Associated Press. 4 Oct. 1988.

38. "Background on Ruth myth" Gustky, Earl. "Point Is, He Didn't: Conference Lays to Rest Myth of Ruth's Called Shot." *Los Angeles Times*. 22 June 1995.

38. "Background on Ruth's called home run" McCarron, Anthony. "75 Years ago Babe Ruth called his famous shot — or did he?" New York *Daily News*. 3 Oct. 2007.

41. "Tug McGraw obituary." Litzky, Frank. "Tug McGraw, 59, star with Mets and Phillies, Dies." *The New York Times*. 6 Jan. 2004.

42. "Schilling on Yankees." Lelinwalla, Mark and McShane, Larry. "Schilling rips New York fans, says Yankees (stink)." New York *Daily News*. 9 Sept. 2008.

42. "Curt Schilling on being hated." "They Said It." *Sports Illustrated*. 6 March 2006.

42. "History of LCS trash talk." Harper, John. "Mastering Art of Cool." New York *Daily News*. 11 Oct. 2001.

43. "Looking back at Terry's remark." Copp, Earle. "Copp's Beat." *Free-lance Star*. 9 Sept. 1953.

CHAPTER 3

44. "Harry Caray's obituary." Sandomir, Richard. "Harry Caray, 78, Colorful Baseball Announcer Dies." *The New York Times*. 19 Feb. 1998.

44. "Harry Caray's Funeral" Bluth, Andrew. "Harry Caray Remembered as Baseball Ambassador." *The New York Times*. 28 Feb. 1998.

47. "Look back at Lou Brock trade." "Lou Brock, A Rock of Ages, hits No. 3000." *Miami News*. 14 Aug. 1979.

48. "Whitey Herzog on Ryne Sandberg." Van Dyck, Dick. "Baby Ruth Cub MVP, Bar None." *The Chicago Tribune*. 29 Sept. 1989.

49. "Background on Alexander" "Cardinals claim Alexander by Waiver Route from Cubs." *The Evening Independent*. 23 June 1926.

49. "Background on Alexander." "Grover Cleveland Alexander." Published at Encyclopedia.com. 2004.

50. "Baker-La Russa history." Ratto, Ray. "Bad Blood Boils like it's the '80s." *San Francisco Chronicle*. 10 Oct. 2002.

50. "Baker-La Russa background." Muskat, Carrie. "Meeting of the Minds." Published at MLB.com. 4 Sept. 2003.

50. "Baker-La Russa history." "Benches clear in Cardinals-Reds Game." *The New York Times*. 11 Aug. 2010.

53. "The trade of Bruce Sutter." "Cards get Sutter." United Press International. 10 Dec. 1980.

57. "McGwire, Sosa Home Run Chase." Verducci, Tom. "The Greatest Season Ever." *Sports Illustrated*. 5 Oct. 1998.

CHAPTER 4

59. "Duke Snider Obituary." Brown, Emma. "Duke Snider Dies." *The Washington Post*. 27 Feb. 2011.

59. "Willie Mays, Duke Snider, Mickey Mantle Background." MacDonald, Ian. "Mays Says It's Time to Put Duke in Hall." *Montreal Gazette*. 9 Jan. 1973.

59. "Background on CF stars." "Duke of Flatbush Joins Mantle, Mays." The Associated Press. 4 Aug. 1980.

59. "Duke Snider Obituary." Goldstein, Richard and Weber, Bruce. "Duke Snider, A Prince of New York's Golden Age of Baseball, Dies at 84." *The New York Times*. 28 Feb. 2011.

60. "Reliving Pine Tar Game." Madden, Bill. "Goose Cooks Hall of a Class." New York *Daily News*. 21 July 1999.

61. "Background on Smokey Joe Williams, Cannonball Redding" Lacy, Sam. "Educating One of Baseball's Better Minds." *Baltimore Afro-American*. 28 June 1997.

61. "Background on Smokey Joe Williams, Cannonball Redding." "Player Pages." Published at NegroLeagueBaseballPlayersAssociation.com. 2000–2007.

62. "Details of Tommy Lasorda, Phanatic." "Phanatic, Lasorda feuding." The Associated Press. 19 July 1991.

63. "Dizzy Dean on his bravado." Okrent, Daniel and Wulf, Steve. *Baseball Anecdotes*. New York: Oxford, 1989.

63. "Dizzy Dean passes away." *Los Angeles Times*. 19 July 1974.

63. "Background on Satchel Paige." "Indians sign Satchel Paige." The Associated Press. 8 July 1948.

63. "Background on Satchel Paige." "Satchel Paige, Negro Ballplayer, is one of the best pitchers in the Game." *LIFE*. 2 June 1941.

63. "Background on Satchel Paige." Okrent, Daniel and Wulf, Steve. *Baseball Anecdotes*. New York: Oxford, 1989.

65. "Background on DiMaggio-Williams trade talk." "The Deals that Baseball Didn't Make." United Press International. 31 Jan. 1966.

67. "The magical 1912 season of Smoky Joe Wood, Walter Johnson." Okrent, Daniel and Wulf, Steve. *Baseball Anecdotes*. New York: Oxford, 1989.

69. "Background on Josh Gibson." "Player Pages." Published at NegroLeagueBaseballPlayersAssociation.com. 2000–2007.

70. "The passing of Wilbert Robinson." "Bath Tub Fall Fatal to Wilbert Robinson." United Press International. 9 Aug. 1934.

71. "Nolan Ryan, Robin Ventura background." Wulf, Steve. "Basebrawl." *Sports Illustrated*. 16 Aug. 1993.

73. "Billy Martin's obituary." Chass, Murray. "Billy Martin of the Yankees Killed in Crash on Icy Road." *The New York Times*. 26 Dec. 1989.

74. "The legacy of Charles O. Finley." "ESPN SportsCentury: Charles Finley." Published at ESPN.com. 2007.

74. "Charles Finley, Bowie Kuhn feud." "Finley Takes Kuhn Fight To Court." The Associated Press. 1 Dec. 1973.

74. "Charles Finley, Bowie Kuhn feud." "Kuhn, Finley feud on Sale of Player." The Associated Press. 25 Feb. 1977.

75. "Branch Rickey talks about his life in baseball." Holland, Gerald. "Mr. Rickey and The Game." *Sports Illustrated*. 7 March 1955.

75. "Life of Branch Rickey." "Branch Rickey, 83, dies in Missouri." United Press International. 10 Dec. 1965.

76. "Background on Phil Rizzuto, Pee Wee Reese." "Fans Argue Abilities of Rizzuto, Reese." The Associated Press. 6 May 1941.

76. "Background on Pee Wee Reese." "Veterans give Hall of Fame nod to Reese." The Associated Press. 5 March 1984.

76. "The Hall of Fame journey for Phil Rizzuto." Jr. Thomas, Robert. "As Lefty, Leo enter, Wait Lifted for Scooter." *The Washington Post*. 1 Aug. 1994.

79. "Background on Nolan Ryan, Steve Carlton." "Rocket's Reaching New Heights." The Associated Press. 24 July 2001.

79. "A Tale of Two pitchers." Okrent, Daniel and Wulf, Steve. *Baseball Anecdotes*. New York: Oxford, 1989.

CHAPTER 5

80. "Sandy Koufax background." Okrent, Daniel and Wulf, Steve. "Sandy Koufax." *Baseball Anecdotes*. New York: Oxford, 1989.

80. "Sandy Koufax after 1963 World Series. "Sandy Wants Most Wins." *St. Petersburg Times*. 9 Oct. 1963.

82. "Red Barber obituary." "Broadcaster Red Barber Dies at 84." The Associated Press. 22 Oct. 1992.

82. "Red Barber's passing." Jr. Thomas, Robert. "Red Barber, Baseball Voice of Summer, is Dead at 84." *The New York Times*. 23 Oct. 1992.

83. "Background on Billy Martin." Okrent, Daniel and Wulf, Steve. "The Triumph of Casey Stengel." *Baseball Anecdotes*. New York: Oxford, 1989.

83. "Billy Martin's catch." "New York Yankees Jubilant, but Heap Praise on Dodgers." The Associated Press. 8 Oct. 1952.

85. "Reggie Jackson on his majestic home runs." Jr. Blount, Ron. "Everyone is Helpless and In Awe." *Sports Illustrated*. 17 June 1974.

87. "Sandy Amoros' million-dollar catch." Jr. Thomas, Robert. "Sandy Amoros, World Series Star for Dodgers in 1955, Dies at 62." *The New York Times*. 28 June 1992.

88. "Don Larsen perfect game background." Okrent, Daniel and Wulf, Steve. "Return to Glory." *Baseball Anecdotes*. New York: Oxford, 1989.

90. "Cookie Lavagetto's big hit." Okrent, Daniel and Wulf, Steve. "The Incredible Series." *Baseball Anecdotes*. New York: Oxford, 1989.

91. "Mickey Owen obituary." Goldstein, Richard. "Mickey Owen Dies at 89." *The New York Times*. 15 July 2005.

93. "Background on Los Angeles Dodgers." Murray, Jim. "Which Way to Chavez Ravine?" *Jim Murray: An Autobiography*. New York: MacMillan, 1993.

93. "History of George Steinbrenner." Madden, Bill. *Steinbrenner*. New York: HarperCollins, 2010.

CHAPTER 6

94. "Robin Ventura's Grand Slam single" Wilkinson, Jack. "NLCS Was One to Be Remembered." Cox News Services. 21 Oct. 1999.

97. "Catching up with Jeffrey Maier." Lapointe, Joe. "Boy Who Helped Yankees is a Hit Again." *The New York Times*. 14 April 2006.

97. "Jeffrey Maier's catch." Weber, Bruce. "Boy Who Saved Yankees Becomes a Man about Town." *The New York Times*. 11 Oct. 1996.

103. "Yankees and Twins." "Yanks sweep Twins, return to ALCS." *Sports Illustrated*. 9 Oct. 2010.

CHAPTER 7

110. "Fielder Jones' obituary." "Fielder Jones is Dead at 62 Years." The Associated Press. 14 March 1934.

111. "Background on 1989 World Series." Martinez, Michael. "One Year Later, Bay Area Fans Still Can't Forget 5:04 p.m." *The New York Times*. 18 Oct. 1990.

111. "Athletics-Giants' history lesson." "Giants, A's hardly rivals." The Associated Press. 2 July 1997.

112. "Clemens-Piazza bat flap." "Benches clear as Clemens throws broken bat at Piazza." Published at CNNSI.com. 22 Oct. 2000.

115. "Background on 1921–23 World Series." "Giants Have Edge on World's Series." United Press. 3 Oct. 1923.

115. "Reds pitcher's prediction in 1923." Rixey, Eppa. "Reds Twirler Picks Giants to Win in The Big Series." *The Evening Independent*. 6 Oct. 1923.

116. "Willie Mays Catch." "Mays Still No. 1" *The Hour*. 15 July 1985.

117. "Background on Ty Cobb." Stanton, Tom. *Ty And The Babe*. New York: Thomas Dunne Books, 2007.

118. "Background on Athletics-Giants' World Series." "Chief Bender Dies at 71." The Associated Press. 23 May 1954.

119. "Background on St. Louis Browns' defensive miscues." "Poor Fielding Costs Browns World Series." United Press International. 10 Oct. 1944.

119. "The Cardinals deserving World Series." "Best Club, St. Louis Cardinals, Win 1944 World Series Crown." The Associated Press. 10 Oct. 1944.

CHAPTER 8

120. "Brandon Phillips lashes out." McCoy, Hal. "Reds 2B Brandon Phillips: 'I Hate the Cardinals.'" *The Sporting News*. 10 Aug 2010.

120. "Background on Reds, Cardinals' flap." Schoenfield, David. "Reds-Cardinals baseball's best rivalry." Published at ESPN.com. 16 May 2011.

122. "Fred Merkle background." "Merkle's Boner." Published at Inhistoric.com. 23 Sept. 2010.

122. "Fred Merkle Obituary." "Fred Merkle, 67, Ballplayer Dies." *The New York Times*. 3 March 1956.

123. "Negro League history." Riley, James. *The Biographical Encyclopedia of the Negro Baseball Leagues*. New York: Carroll & Graf Publishers, Inc., 1994.

123. "Background on Chicago American Giants, Kansas City Monarchs." Gay, Timothy. *Satch, Dizzy & Rapid Robert*. New York: Simon & Schuster, 2001.

123. "Background on Negro Leagues." "Teams and Leagues." Published at NLMB.com. Negro League Museum. 1994.

125. "Background on Greatest Pennant Race Ever." James, Bill. "Pennant Races of the 1890s." *The New Bill James Historical Abstract*. New York: Free Press, 2001.

128. "Background on Armando Benitez brawl." Curry, Jack. "Benitez again Holds Ball, and Martinez Has the Bat." *The New York Times*. 5 June 1999.

128. "Background on Armando Benitez brawl." "Put Up Your Dukes." Published at ESPN.com. 2008.

131. "Chipper Jones' success against the Mets." Bierman, Fred. "Fab Four and More." *The New York Times*. 27 Sept. 2008.

131. "Background Shea and Chipper names." "So long, Shea: Mets Close Shop after 45 Years." The Associated Press. 27 Sept. 2008.

132. "The Phillies–Pirates' rivalry of the 1970s." "Phils Laud Feisty Pirates." The Associated Press. 2 Oct. 1978.

135. "The Cardinals-Dodgers of the 1940s." "St. Louis Cardinals are 1946 National Baseball League Pennant Winners." The Associated Press. 4 Oct. 1946.

135. "The Cardinals-Dodgers of the 1940s." "Durocher Confident Cards Will Crack." United Press International. 6 Sept. 1946.

136. "Tigers–Blue Jays race." "Jays Don't Feel They Choked Down the Stretch." United Press International. 5 Oct. 1987.

CHAPTER 9

139. "The Shot Heard Round the World." Hirsch, James. *Willie Mays: The Life, The Legend*. New York: Scribner, 2010.

140. "Background on Steve Finley and the Dodgers." Jenkins, Lee. "Dodgers Win West With a Late Grand Slam." *The New York Times*. 3 Oct. 2004.

141. "Keys to the Dodgers' 1959 season." "Maury Wills Ends Illustrious Career." The Associated Press. 4 June 1969.

141. "Background on Giants' collapse." "Giants' Fall Controversy Stirs Again." United Press International. 7 March 1961.

141. "Giants knock out Dodgers in 1982." "Morgan Agrees To Contract With A's." The Associated Press. 13 Dec. 1983.

141. "Joe Morgan's memorable home run." "Atlanta Gains Playoffs." The Associated Press. 4 Oct. 1982.

142. "Background on Don Drysdale, Orel Hershiser streaks" Street, Jim. "Sele hits, ump misses?" Published at MLB.com. 30 April. 2005.

142. "Background on Don Drysdale, Orel Hershiser streaks" "Hershiser Didn't Want The Record." The Associated Press. 30 Sept. 1988.

145. "Looking back on 1962 finish." "Frisco Site of Series." The Associated Press. 4 Oct. 1962.

145. "Background on final 1962 weekend." "Trailing by 2 Runs, Giants Score 4 in Ninth." United Press International. 5 Oct. 1962.

146. "The secret to the 1965 Dodgers." "Determination the Key to Dodgers' Success." The Associated Press. 5 Oct. 1965.

148. "Dodgers ruin opening of Giants' new park." "Elster Has Ball at Giants' Expense." The Associated Press. 12 April 2000.

149. "Juan Marichal clubs John Roseboro with bat." "Put Up Your Dukes." Published at ESPN.com. 2008.

151. "The big finish to the 1997 season." "Johnson Delivers Latest Dramatic Home Run in Giants-Dodgers' Rivalry." The Associated Press. 19 Sept. 1997.

152. "Barry Bonds' single-season home run record." "Bonds Breaks Home Run Record." The Associated Press. 7 Oct. 2001.

152. "Barry Bonds' home run record." Rubin, Adam. "Bonds Breaks Record." New York *Daily News*. 7 Oct. 2001.

154. "Salomon Torres' fateful start vs. Dodgers." Moore, David Leon. "Baker Gambles, Loses on Torres." *USA Today*. 4 Oct. 1993.

155. "Jackie Robinson's exit from the game." "Giants Unable to Talk Jackie into Returning." United Press International. 7 Jan. 1957.

CREDITS

OTTO GREULE JR./GETTY IMAGES: Cover (Johnson); 7 (Martinez); 24; 150-151
JOHN GRIESHOP/MLB PHOTOS: Cover (Phillips); 121
RICH PILLING/MLB PHOTOS: Cover (Red Sox); 2-3; 6 (Lee); 7 (Sutter); 17; 29; 30; 35; 40; 53; 54; 62 (2); 78; 79; 108; 112-113; 152-153
NBLA/MLB PHOTOS: Cover (Jackson); 6 (Durocher); 7 (Mays); 8; 10; 11; 16; 33; 36; 43; 49; 58; 59; 61; 64; 65; 66; 67; 84; 110; 118; 123; 130
JONATHAN DANIEL/GETTY IMAGES: Back Cover (Baker and LaRussa); 37; 50-51
MLB PHOTOS: Back Cover (A's); 7 (Boggs); 13; 74 (Kuhn); 111; 141 (Morgan)
FRANK SCHERSCHEL/TIME & LIFE PICTURES/GETTY IMAGES: 14
BRUCE BENNETT STUDIOS/GETTY IMAGES: 15; 60; 149
FOCUS ON SPORT/GETTY IMAGES: 18; 73; 74 (Finley); 106-107; 142; 147
DICK RAPHAEL/SPORTS ILLUSTRATED/GETTY IMAGES: 20
FRANCES ROBERTS/AP PHOTO: 21
EZRA SHAW/GETTY IMAGES: 22-23; 104-105
DOUG PENSINGER/GETTY IMAGES: 26; 42
JED JACOBSOHN/GETTY IMAGES: 28; 148
BRAD MANGIN/MLB PHOTOS: 34
MARK RUCKER/TRANSCENDENTAL GRAPHICS/GETTY IMAGES: 38-39; 63; 68-69; 114-115; 117; 122; 125; 138-139; 155
JON SOOHOO/MLB PHOTOS: 44-45
LOUIS REQUENA/MLB PHOTOS: 46-47; 59 (Mantle); 72; 100
RONALD C. MODRA/SPORTS IMAGERY/GETTY IMAGES: 48; 92-93
HAROLD FILAN/AP PHOTO: 52
RON VESELY/MLB PHOTOS: 55
PETER NEWCOMB/AFP/GETTY IMAGES: 56
ROGERS PHOTO ARCHIVE/GETTY IMAGES: 70; 134-135
LINDA KAYE/AP PHOTO: 71
SPORTING NEWS ARCHIVE/GETTY IMAGES: 75
KIDWILER COLLECTION/DIAMOND IMAGES/GETTY IMAGES: 77
HERB SCHARFMAN/SPORTS IMAGERY/GETTY IMAGES: 81
DAVID McLANE/NY DAILY NEWS ARCHIVE/GETTY IMAGES: 82
DIAMOND IMAGES/GETTY IMAGES: 83; 89; 102
FRANK HURLEY/NY DAILY NEWS ARCHIVE/GETTY IMAGES: 86-87
BILL MEURER/NY DAILY NEWS ARCHIVE/GETTY IMAGES: 90
BOB SEELIG/NY DAILY NEWS ARCHIVE/GETTY IMAGES: 91
HOWARD EARL SIMMONS/NY DAILY NEWS ARCHIVE/GETTY IMAGES: 94-95
ROBERT SULLIVAN/AFP/GETTY IMAGES: 96
LINDA CATAFFO/NY DAILY NEWS ARCHIVE/GETTY IMAGES: 97
STEPHEN DUNN/GETTY IMAGES: 98-99; 126-127; 140
AL BELLO/GETTY IMAGES: 103; 131
NY DAILY NEWS ARCHIVE/GETTY IMAGES: 116
AP PHOTO: 119; 144-145
JOHN DOMINIS/TIME & LIFE PICTURES/GETTY IMAGES: 124
TODD WARSHAW/GETTY IMAGES: 129
BILL PIERCE/TIME & LIFE PICTURES/GETTY IMAGES: 132-133
GRAY MORTIMORE/GETTY IMAGES: 136
MICHAEL ZAGARIS/MLB PHOTOS: 137
GEORGE SILK/TIME & LIFE PICTURES/GETTY IMAGES: 141 (Wills)
PHOTO FILE/MLB PHOTOS: 143
BERNSTEIN ASSOCIATES/GETTY IMAGES: 154

INDEX

Agbayani, Benny, 112
Aerosmith, 57
Alderson, Sandy, 118
Alexander, Doyle, 136
Alexander, Pete Grover, 49
Ali, Muhammad, 9
Allen, Mel, 82
Alomar, Roberto, 128
Alou, Felipe, 57, 140, 145
Alston, Walt, 146
Altrock, Nick, 110
Alvarez, Wilson, 151
Amoros, Sandy, 87
Anderson, Brady, 128
Anderson, Sparky, 136
Andrews, Mike, 74
Andujar, Joaquin, 109
Arizona Diamondbacks, 29, 42, 140
Arlington Stadium, 71
Ashburn, Richie, 80
Associated Press, 146
Atlanta Braves, 12, 54, 94, 96, 131, 141, 142, 154
Arroyo, Bronson, 29, 120
Baker, Dusty, 50, 120, 141, 151, 154
Baker, Frank, 118
Baltimore Orioles, 70, 88, 97, 100, 106, 110, 119, 125, 128
Banks, Ernie, 44, 123
Barber, Red, 32, 82
Barry, Jack, 118
Baseball Anecdotes, 122
Bavasi, Buzzy, 155
Baylor, Don, 79, 94

Bearden, Gene, 14
Beck, Rod, 154
Bell, George, 136
Belle, Albert, 105
Beltran, Carlos, 35
Bench, Johnny, 106, 124
Bender, Chief, 118
Benitez, Armando, 128
Bergman, Dave, 136
Berra, Yogi, 73, 83, 87
Bevens, Bill, 90
Blair, Paul, 73
Blue, Vida, 74, 101
Boggs, Wade, 12
Bonds, Barry, 50, 96, 148, 151, 152
Bonilla, Bobby, 96, 97
Boone, Aaron, 27
Boston Beaneaters, 125
Boston Braves, 14
Boston Globe, 9
Boston Red Sox, 9, 11, 12, 14, 15, 16, 17, 18, 20, 21, 23, 25, 27, 28, 31, 54, 65, 67, 74, 76, 99, 105
Bowa, Larry, 132
Boys of Summer, 59
Branca, Ralph, 139, 141
Bream, Sid, 96
Brennaman, Marty, 120
Brett, George, 60, 102
Bridwell, Al, 122
Brock, Lou, 47, 53
Broglio, Ernie, 47
Brooklyn Dodgers, 32, 43, 59, 61, 70, 75, 76, 80, 82, 83, 87, 88, 90, 91, 135,
139, 155
Brown, Kevin, 31
Brush, John, 118
Buckner, Bill, 12, 124
Bunyan, Paul, 69
Burleson, Rick, 20
Busch Stadium, 109
Butler, Brett, 142
Cabrera, Francisco, 96
Candlestick Park, 59, 111, 141, 151
California Angels, 71
Campanella, Roy, 88
Caray, Harry, 44
Cardwell, Don, 52
Carey, Max, 43
Carlton, Steve, 79, 132
Carpenter, Chris, 120
Carter, Gary, 126
Casey, Hugh, 91
Cashen, Frank, 37
Cepeda, Orlando, 141
Cey, Ron, 93, 124
Chambliss, Chris, 102
Chance, Frank, 110
Chandler, Happy, 32
Chavez Ravine, 154
Chesbro, Jack, 11
Chicago American Giants, 123
Chicago Cubs, 21, 38, 44, 47, 48, 49, 50, 52, 53, 57, 110, 120, 122
Chicago Tribune, 47, 48
Chicago White Sox, 44, 71, 110, 119, 151
Cincinnati Reds, 17, 50, 94, 101, 106, 120, 124, 142, 146

Cinderella, 119
Clark, Jack, 109
Clark, Will, 111
Clemens, Roger, 23, 25
Cleveland Indians, 17, 71, 105, 116, 130
Cobb, Ty, 61, 117
Coleman, Jerry, 15
Collins, Eddie, 118
Columbia University, 11
Comiskey, Charles, 110
Comiskey Park, 44
Cone, David, 37
Cordero, Francisco, 120
Cox, Billy, 83
Cuellar, Mike, 101
Cueto, Johnny, 120
Craig, Roger, 141
Damon, Johnny, 31
Dark, Alvin, 145
Darwin, Danny, 151
Davenport, Jim, 145
Denkinger, Don, 109
Dent, Bucky, 20, 27
Dean, Dizzy, 63, 69
Detroit Tigers, 136, 151
Dibble, Rob, 17
Dietz, Dick, 142
DiMaggio, Joe, 16, 65, 91
Dobson, Pat, 101
Doby, Larry, 116
Doubleday, Abner, 36
Drysdale, Don, 141, 142, 146
Dugan, Joe, 11
Duke University, 9

Duquette, Dan, 25
Durham, Leon, 53
Durocher, Leo, 32, 75, 135, 139
Dykstra, Lenny, 126
Ebbets Field, 75, 91
Eckersley, Dennis, 111
Elster, Kevin, 148
Erickson, Scott, 128
Erskine, Carl, 80
Evans, Dwight, 17
Evers, Johnny, 110, 122
Fairly, Ron, 149
Feller, Bob, 14, 116
Fenway Park, 25, 28, 29, 67, 73, 99
Fingers, Rollie, 74
Finley, Charles, 74
Finley, Steve, 140
Fisk, Carlton, 17
Florida Marlins, 35
Forbes Field, 117
Ford, Whitey, 80, 87
Forster, Terry, 141
Foster, George, 106
Foster, Rube, 123
Fox Sports Midwest, 120
Franklin, Wayne, 140
Franks, Herman, 146
Francona, Terry, 27
Frazee, Harry, 9, 11
Frazier, Joe, 9
Furillo, Carl, 83, 88, 90
Garcia, Rich, 97
Gardenhire, Ron, 103
Garvey, Steve, 85, 93
Gehrig, Lou, 11, 49
Gibson, Bob, 142
Gibson, Josh, 69
Gibson, Kirk, 140
Gionfriddo, Al, 90
Giusti, Dave, 106
Gonzalez, Luis, 42
Gooden, Dwight, 126
Goodfellas, 62
Good Morning America, 97
Gordon, Joe, 91
Gossage, Goose, 20, 60
Green Monster, 20
Green, Shawn, 140
Griffin, Alfredo, 142
Griffith, Clark, 67
Gross, Kevin, 154
Guerrero, Pedro, 93, 141
Guidry, Ron, 18, 20
Guthrie, Mark, 151
Gutteridge, Don, 119
Hall of Fame, 12, 48, 53, 60, 65, 76, 82, 110, 116, 117, 119, 120, 146, 155
Hamels, Cole, 35
Hargrove, Mike, 71
Henderson, Rickey, 47, 111
Henrich, Tommy, 91
Herman, Billy, 135
Hermanson, Dustin, 140
Hernandez, Keith, 126
Hernandez, Roberto, 151
Hershiser, Orel, 142
Herzog, Whitey, 48, 109, 126
Hilltop Park, 11

Historical Baseball Abstract, 125
Hobson, Butch, 18
Hodges, Gil, 87
Hodges, Russ, 139
Hollywood, Calif., 15, 140
Holtzman, Ken, 101
Homestead Grays, 61, 69
Hooton, Burt, 85
Hough, Charlie, 85
Houston Astros, 71, 142
Howard, Elston, 73
Howser, Dick, 109
Hoyt, Waite, 11
Hunter, Catfish, 74, 101, 102
Hyatt Wilshire, 93
Isbell, Frank, 110
Jackson, Danny, 109
Jackson, Reggie, 73, 83, 85, 93, 101
James, Bill, 125
Jeter, Derek, 27, 97, 112, 128
Johnson, Brian, 151
Johnson, Byron, 130
Johnson, Lou, 146
Johnson, Randy, 42, 61, 67
Johnson, Walter, 61, 79
Jones, Andruw, 54, 94
Jones, Chipper, 94, 131
Jones, Fielder, 110
Jones, Sheldon, 139
Jorgensen, Spider, 90
Kaat, Jim, 132
Kahn, Roger, 59
Kansas City Monarchs, 69, 123
Kansas City Royals, 60, 102, 109
Keeler, Wee Willie, 125
Keller, Charlie, 91
Kennedy, Bob, 53
Kenmore Square, 20
Key, Jimmy, 128
Koenig, Mark, 38
Koufax, Sandy, 80, 146, 148, 149
Kramer, Jack, 14
Kinder, Ellis, 14
Kuhn, Bowie, 59, 74
Kurowksi, George, 119
Kuzava, Bob, 83
Lajoie, Nap, 130
Lanier, Max, 119
Lansdowne Street, 20
Lansford, Carney, 111
Larsen, Don, 88, 90
La Rue, Jason, 120
La Russa, Tony, 50, 120
Lasorda, Tommy, 37, 62, 80, 93, 142
Lavagetto, Cookie, 90
Lee, Bill, 17
Lee, Derrek, 54
Lemon, Bob, 14, 116
Leonard, Jeffrey, 111
Leyland, Jim, 96
Lincoln Memorial, 71
Lindell, Johnny, 15
Little, Grady, 23, 27
Littlefield, Dick, 155
Live With Regis & Kathie Lee, 97
Lofton, Kenny, 105
Lopes, Davey, 93, 124
Lopez, Al, 116

Long, Herman, 125
Look (magazine), 155
Los Angeles Angels, 99
Los Angeles Dodgers, 28, 37, 62, 73, 80, 85, 93, 124, 140, 141, 145, 146, 148, 149, 154
Los Angeles Times, 75
Lowe, Derek, 31
Lowrie, Jed, 99
Lucchino, Larry, 9
Mack, Connie, 36, 118, 130
MacPhail, Larry, 135
Maier, Jeffrey, 97
Mantle, Mickey, 57, 59, 80, 83, 88, 131
Marion, Marty, 119
Marsh, Randy, 29
Marichal, Juan, 149
Maris, Roger, 57
Martin, Billy, 60, 73, 80, 83, 85
Martinez, Pedro, 23, 25, 27, 105
Mathewson, Christy, 115, 118, 122
Matsui, Hideki, 27,
Mays, Carl, 11
Mays, Willie, 59, 116, 139, 145, 146, 152
McCarthy, Joe, 14, 15
McClelland, Tim, 60
McCormick, Moose, 122
McCovey, Willie, 142, 145
McDougald, Gil, 88
McFerrin, Bobby, 148
McGlinchy, Kevin, 94
McGraw, John, 36, 70, 115, 118, 125, 130
McGraw, Tug, 41
McGwire, Mark, 57
McInnis, Stuffy, 118
McLain, Denny, 11
McNally, Dave, 101
Medwick, Joe, 135
Merkle, Fred, 122
Millar, Kevin, 28
Miller, Ray, 128
Minnesota Twins, 103
Mirabelli, Doug, 148
Mitchell, Dale, 88
Moeller, Danny, 67
Molina, Yadier, 120
Montreal Expos, 23, 57, 142
Montville, Leigh, 38
Moose, Bob, 106
Morgan, Joe, 106, 124, 141, 154
Moryn, Walt, 52
Mount Rushmore, 65
Mueller, Bill, 28
Mulliniks, Rance, 136
Munson, Thurman, 17, 73
Murray, Eddie, 105
Murray, Jim 75
Musial, Stan, 44, 119
Mussina, Mike, 128
MVP Award, 16, 48, 76, 85, 131, 136
Negro Leagues, 61, 63, 69, 123, 155
Negro Leagues Players Association, 61
Nelson, Jeff, 112
Nettles, Graig, 17
Newcombe, Don, 139
New York *Daily News*, 37
New York Giants, 32, 36, 43, 59, 70, 75, 116, 118, 122, 139, 142

New York Highlanders, 11
New York Mets, 12, 35, 37, 41, 94, 112, 126, 128, 132, 146
New York Times, 82, 139
New York Yankees, 9, 11, 12, 14, 15, 16, 17, 18, 20, 21, 23, 25, 27, 28, 29, 31, 32, 42, 59, 60, 65, 73, 75, 76, 80, 82, 83, 85, 87, 88, 90, 91, 93, 102, 103, 105, 112, 115, 128, 135, 139
Nichols, Kid, 125
Nintendo, 23
Oakland Athletics, 44, 50, 74, 85, 100, 106, 111, 118
Ohio State University, 9
O'Day, Hank, 122
O'Malley, Walter, 75, 82
O'Neil, Buck, 69, 123
Orta, Jorge, 109
Ortiz, David, 21, 28, 31, 99
Ott, Mel, 32
Owen, Dave, 48
Owen, Mickey, 91
Pacific Bell Park, 148
Paige, Satchel, 61, 63, 69
Palmer, Jim, 101
Palmeiro, Rafael, 128
Park, Chan Ho, 152
Parker, Dave, 132
Pearl Harbor, 16
Pedroia, Dustin, 76
Patek, Fred, 76
Philadelphia Athletics, 36, 118, 130
Philadelphia Phillies, 23, 35, 41, 52, 130, 132, 136, 139
Phillips, Brandon, 120
Piazza, Mike, 94
Pierce, Billy, 145
Piniella, Lou, 17, 20
Pistons, Detroit, 125
Pittsburgh Pirates, 75, 79, 94, 96, 106, 117, 132
Podres, Johnny, 141, 146
Polo Grounds, 115, 118, 122, 139, 145, 151
Posada, Jorge, 23, 27
Pratt, Todd, 94
Pujols, Albert, 54, 120
Ramirez, Manny, 23, 99, 105
Randolph, Willie, 102
Ransom, Cody, 140
Rawlings, Johnny, 115
Reagan, Ronald, 44
Redding, Dick, 61
Reese, Pee Wee, 76, 87, 135
Reiser, Pete, 90
Reitz, Ken, 53
Remy, Jerry, 20, 27
Reuss, Jerry, 141
Rhodes, Dusty, 116
Rice, Grantland, 115
Rice, Jim, 20, 73
Rickey, Branch, 75, 135
Rigney, Bill, 141
Riles, Ernest, 142
Ripken, Cal, Jr., 128
Ripple, Jimmy, 69
Rivera, Mariano, 27, 28, 112

Rivers, Mickey, 17
Rixey, Eppa, 115
Rizzuto, Phil, 76
Roberts, Dave, 28, 31
Robinson, Jackie, 32, 61, 75, 76, 83, 88, 123, 155
Robinson, Wilbert, 70
Rodgers, Buck, 71
Rodriguez, Alex, 29
Roebuck, Ed, 145
Rogers, Kenny, 94
Rohe, George, 110
Rollins, Jimmy 35
Root, Charlie, 38
Rose, Pete, 106, 124
Roseboro, John, 149
Rudi, Joe, 74
Ruffing, Red, 11
Russell, Bill, 93
Ruth, Babe, 9, 11, 20, 21, 23, 38, 49, 57, 61, 85, 115, 117
Ryan, Nolan, 61, 71, 79
St. Louis Browns, 119
St. Louis Cardinals, 31, 43, 44, 47, 48, 49, 50, 52, 53, 54, 57, 75, 119, 120, 126, 135
Saberhagen, Bret, 109
Sandberg, Ryne, 48
San Diego Padres, 136, 142
San Francisco Giants, 50, 111, 112, 118, 140, 141, 148, 149, 151, 154, 155
Santana, Johan, 103
Saturday Evening Post, 91

Schilling, Curt, 29, 32, 42
Schmidt, Mike, 132
Scully, Vin, 82
Seals Stadium, 141
Seattle Mariners, 17
Sewell, Luke, 119
Shantz, Bobby, 47
Shaughnessy, Dan, 9
Shea Stadium, 94, 112, 131
Shotton, Burt, 90
Sierra Club, 35
Smith, Red, 139
Snider, Duke, 59, 76, 80, 83
Snow, J.T., 148
Sosa, Elias, 85
Sosa, Sammy, 57
Southworth, Billy, 119
Sport (magazine), 73
Sportsman's Park, 119
Stahl, Jake, 67
Stanky, Eddie, 90
Stargell, Willie, 79, 132
Steinbrenner, George, 14, 73, 85, 93, 112
Stengel, Casey, 43, 59, 65, 83
Stephens, Vernon, 119
Strawberry, Darryl, 126
Sutter, Bruce, 48, 53
Sutton, Don, 124
"Take Me Out To the Ballgame," 44
Tampa Bay Rays, 35
Tanana, Frank, 136
Tanner, Chuck, 132
Tarasco, Tony, 97

The Beatles, 62
"The Curse of Bambino," 9
Thome, Jim, 105
Terry, Bill, 43
Texas Rangers, 71
The Sporting News, 125
Thomson, Bobby, 139, 141, 148
Tinker, Joe, 110
Topping, Dan, 65
Toronto Blue Jays, 25, 109, 136
Torre, Joe, 112, 128
Torres, Salomon, 154
Torrez, Mike, 20
Tracy, Jim, 140, 152
Trammell, Alan, 136
Trillo, Manny, 74
Union Park, 125
United States, 16
United Press International, 119
University of North Carolina, 9
University of Michigan, 9
Valentin, John, 25
Valentine, Bobby, 112
Valenzuela, Fernando, 93, 141
Van Slyke, Andy, 96
Vazquez, Javier, 31
Veeck, Bill, 48, 63
Ventura, Robin, 71, 94
Veterans Stadium, 62
Waddell, Rube, 130
Wagner, Honus, 117
Wakefield, Tim, 27
Walker, Rube, 139

Wall Street Journal, 139
Walsh, Ed, 110
Washington Nationals, 35
Washington Senators, 67
Weaver, Earl, 110
Welch, Bob, 141
Werth, Jayson, 140
Wertz, Vic, 116
Wesleyan College, 97
West, Joe, 28
WGN, 44
Whitaker, Lou, 136
Wilkinson, J.L., 123
Williams, Bernie, 27, 112
Williams, Joe Smokey, 61
Williams, Ted, 14, 65, 76
Williams, Stan, 145
Wills, Maury, 141, 145, 149
Wilson, Enrique, 27
Wilson, Willie, 102, 109
Wood, Joe Smoky, 67
Worrell, Todd, 109
Wrigley Field, 17, 38, 44, 48, 52
Wynn, Early, 116
Yankee Stadium, 21, 23, 42, 69, 85, 97
Yastrzemski, Carl, 18, 20, 54
Yawkey, Tom, 14, 15, 65
Yeager, Steve, 93
Young, Cy, 25, 103, 105
Zimmer, Don, 18, 23